"Larry Dugger's book [...] ion, real-life inspiration and bibli[...] [...] an anointed writer and most humble heart. You will be richer for having read it."
—Rebecca Keener, host *Always More TV* and author

"In *Unshakable!* Larry Dugger assures his readers that while we sometimes 'can't see what God is doing,' we can always trust him to give us strength as we face difficult situations. Dugger uses Scripture and skillful storytelling in his quest to help people leave worry and walk into hope. Buy a copy for yourself and a friend; you both will be glad that you did."
—Dr. Mark T. Goodman, author of *The Ordinary Way* and senior pastor of Rabbit Creek Church in Anchorage, Alaska

"*Unshakable!* is not just for the laity, I would highly recommend this material for those in ministry as well. Being a pastor for over twenty-eight years, I have learned how to 'lead while you bleed,' but the wisdom and insight that I found in *Unshakable!* STOPPED the bleeding in many areas of my life."
—Pastor Zack Parr, Solid Rock Church, Kennett, Missouri

"If you struggle with anxiety, stress, or fear, this book was written for you. Larry covers a variety of topics, such as: loneliness, forgiveness, prayer, grace, death, and more. *Unshakable!* helps the reader keep their hope in God and their emotions in check during life's darkest moments. This will be a book you will read over and over."
—Pastor Randy Cowart, City Church, Auburn/Opelika, Alabama

"Larry Dugger's new book, *Unshakable!: A 40-Day Guide to Overcoming Anxiety, Worry, and Emotional Distress*, captures the art of storytelling. Each devotion is drizzled with hope and encourages the reader to expect good things in their future. This encouraging read is hard to put down."
—Tracey Mitchell, author, TV host, and international speaker

"*Unshakable!* brings solid truth to a world that stands on unstable ground. World events and personal struggles threaten our lives and

FIDELIS PUBLISHING

ISBN: 978-1-7358563-8-4
ISBN 978-1-7358563-9-1 (eBook):

Unshakable!
A 40-Day Guide to Overcoming Anxiety, Worry, and Emotional Distress
© 2021 Larry Dugger

Cover Design by Diana Lawrence
Interior Design by LParnell Book Services

For information about special discounts for bulk purchases, please contact BulkBooks.com, call 1-888-959-5153 or email – cs@bulkbooks.com.

Fidelis Publishing, LLC Sterling, VA • Nashville, TN fidelispublishing.com

Manufactured in the United States of America

10 9 8 7 6 5 4 3 2 1

To everyone who's struggling . . .

Contents

Introduction

LIGHTNING STREAKS ACROSS the sky like an Olympic sprinter. Thunder rattles the windows. Rain, like the beating hooves of a hundred horses, crashes down just above your head. The atmosphere is primed for the worst. Your stomach tightens as the vicious storm wraps itself around you. You're uneasy and nervous. In an instant it happens. Someone opens the door and invites the darkness inside. The lights go out . . .

It's one thing when a storm knocks out the lights in your home—it's another when the lights go out in life. Periodically, you will experience blocks of time I describe as emotional, and even spiritual **blackout**—this is when life goes dark due to unforeseen circumstances beyond your control. During a blackout, you're extremely vulnerable and can be overtaken by anxiety, worry, and despair. However, contrary to what you may believe, the darkness is not the problem or the source of what's got you shaking in your boots—it's the fact you can't see what God is doing. The next 40 days are vital because you can lose years of your life if you continue to entertain worrisome thoughts and dismiss your contribution to full recovery. As you read, keep in mind, a blackout is anything that stirs up chaos or confusion in your everyday life.

As a pastor and professional Christian counselor, I've spent a lot of time with those who feel stuck in the shadows of stress and apprehension. Interestingly enough, most of them identify themselves as Christians. Some find it surprising that children of the Light can feel trapped in the dark, with a head full of unsettled thoughts. There are even those who would like you to believe the uneasiness experienced while in a dark spot, is no longer a part of your life, after you receive the light of Christ. That is simply not true. While the gloominess of sin is gone, the darkness of circumstances is all too real. Even Jesus, the Light of the world, experienced the kind of blackout that could have potentially reduced a spiritual champion into a non-contender. The disciple Luke best described what happened to Jesus:

> By now it was noon. The whole earth became dark,
> the darkness lasted three hours—a total blackout.
> (Luke 23:44–45b MSG)

During the Son of God's last three hours on the cross, the sun stopped shining and darkness covered the whole land. Jesus had a sun-stopped-shining "moment," and occasionally so will you. The real question is: What will you do? Will you give up and believe life will never be good again? Will you give in to harassing thoughts? Will you allow nervousness and uneasiness to decide the future? Will you play the blame game? Or will you trust God to get you back on course?

As I prepared to write this book, I wanted the information to be authentic. Too often, we're only attracted to the shiny side of Christianity. Don't misunderstand, I love the thrills and chills of an anointed worship band, and some preaching can lift me so high I think my toes are no longer on the ground. That's all well and good, but I need more than to just bask in the rays of a great church service, only to return to the frustration of my problem—and I'm guessing so do you. With that in mind,

I asked a few of my Christian clients, "What was your darkest day? What was the most worrisome thing you've been through? Just tell me the first thing that pops into your head." With their blessing, I will share a few of their most anxious moments. Maybe you can relate.

What was your worst day?

- The day I found out I had cancer
- The day my wife had a miscarriage
- The day my one-year-old granddaughter died during surgery
- The day my parents divorced
- The day my wife and I had to tell our children we were losing our home due to bankruptcy
- The day my five-year-old daughter drowned at Disney
- The day my mom and siblings were murdered
- The day I allowed myself to slip into drug use
- The day my daughter lost her mind for good
- The day my dad died
- The day I was raped
- The day my husband walked out on me and our two sons
- The day I tried to commit suicide
- The day I found out my wife was having an affair
- The day I pulled the trigger.

These are not the usual topics of discussion in the "Newcomers" class at church—fearfulness and emotional distress rarely are. I wrote this book for that reason. Our journey will take us to Golgotha. There, Jesus hung between heaven and earth for six hours. Three of which were in darkness. If you're in darkness, racked with worrisome thoughts, he knows how to turn the lights back on.

What to Expect

A Daily Motivation – This will help you keep putting one foot in front of the other even on the days when it seems easier to give up. Since unsettling circumstances are often scary and draining, you will need a daily dose of encouragement to keep your mind focused on the promises of God and the path forward. I suggest you read this first thing in the morning so you you'll be ready to take on the day.

A Key Verse – Scripture is a floodlight! Use it to illuminate your circumstances. I recommend you either write down the daily verse on an index card and carry it with you or use the internet feature on your cell phone as a way to retrieve each day's information. This way you can keep God's promise in front of you as you go about your usual routine.

A Reflection Journal – At the end of each day, you will be asked a question. Don't be afraid to bleed on the pages. Open your heart and be honest about how you feel. Journaling will also allow you to look back to see how God brought you out of every anxious situation.

A Fear Blocker – The enemy often uses what you're most afraid of as a way to create undue nervousness and unnecessary concern. Jesus, however, can help you use your fears as opportunities to build a more solid relationship with God. Each fear blocker reminds you anxiety doesn't have to be a weight hanging around your neck. Use each day's blocker as a way to retrain your mind by no longer overthinking your problem.

Beacons of Light – After each section, you will find a list of Scriptures explaining how God moves us out of crippling restlessness and into the light of recovery. Read each verse carefully and commit at least one to memory. Over time, you will develop an arsenal of light that can be used to extinguish every worrisome thought.

Stories of Unshakable Faith – In preparation for the writing of the material you're about to read, I interviewed people from across the country who had recently overcome a time of anxiety and emotional despair, due to unforeseen circumstances. You will be encouraged by their stories of faith.

※ ※ ※

PART I
LIFE GOES DARK WHEN THE SUN STOPS SHINING

*It was now about noon, and darkness
came over the whole land until three in the
afternoon, for the sun stopped shining. And
the curtain of the temple was torn in two. Jesus
called out with a loud voice, "Father, into your
hands I commit my spirit." When he had said
this, he breathed his last. (Luke 23:44–46)*

The darkness may have hidden God from you, but don't
worry, it cannot hide you from him.

Help When Life Gets Heavy

DON'T BE AFRAID to feel the weight of the pressure you're under. After all, Jesus felt the heaviness of the cross. Before you can cast your cares to Jesus, you need to know exactly what you're casting. Today, be honest about the problems you're facing. Prepare yourself to challenge your anxiety, by getting real about the way your life is going. This will not be easy, but it's the first step. You can't start winning until you stop losing.

Key Verse: "Carrying his own cross, he went out to the place of the Skull (which in Aramaic is called Golgotha). There they crucified him" (John 19:17–18a).

Jesus was no lightweight when it came to carrying heavy timber. When your dad is a carpenter, you get use to splinters in your back. I am quite sure this wasn't Jesus's first opportunity to hoist a hefty plank of wood onto his shoulders. However, this time, it was different. Jesus wasn't just scratched, he was wounded. Life was about to leave a mark on him.

Somewhere along the route, Simon the Cyrene helped Jesus carry the heavy load. Jesus had a Golgotha moment and it should come as no surprise when you, his follower, have one of your own. There, the timber dug into already open wounds. Exhausted, stressed, concerned, and at the end of his ability to take another step, Jesus found himself in an overwhelmingly dark place. As previously noted, Luke described it like this:

> It was now about noon, and darkness came over the whole land until three in the afternoon, for the sun stopped shining. (Luke 23:44–45a)

I am guessing you haven't seen the sun in a while and you're beginning to wonder when or if daylight will ever come. Life has left you nervous, uneasy, and worried about an uncertain future. If you knew what to do to stop overthinking and calm your sometimes-racing heart, you would have already done it. But since you're at a loss for answers, you've found yourself in a destructive holding pattern. Why don't you take a moment to write down how you feel? What has robbed you of peace of mind? What is making your stomach churn?

For Jesus, the blackout lasted three hours. For you, it might be three months or even three years—maybe more. But Jesus wasn't worried about the outcome. He already knew where the cross was leading him because he had inside information. You, however, often have no way of knowing exactly what the future holds. Worry and anxiety happen when you allow your mind to dwell on difficult times, causing you to see no path forward. When the sun stops shining, you can even be tempted to believe God made a mistake, that perhaps he is napping or taking a break from watching over you. This could not be further from the truth.

God took a black Friday and turned it into a pastel Sunday morning sunrise! Reversing the crucifixion didn't happen overnight—but it did happen. God stands ready to do the same for you if you will trust him with the future, instead of conjuring worst-case scenarios in your mind. This is not the time to step back and allow dark times to decide how the rest of your life is going to go. This is the time to step up and tell the darkness how it's going to go! The Light living in you is greater than the darkness in which you may currently be living. Jesus proclaimed: "The light shines in the darkness, and the darkness has not overcome it" (John 1:5 ESV).

As an outdoor enthusiast, I have spent hours walking through the dark woods on my way to a favorite hunting spot. And even though I often carry a flashlight, it can be a little unnerving, especially on a moonless night. I learned early in life the darkness doesn't change the woods; it does, however, change me. A familiar path during the day can be disorienting and foreign in the dark. It's easy for your mind to play tricks on you when all you can see are images instead of clearly defined landmarks.

It's time to put "it" in God's hands.

During his three hours on the cross, Jesus somehow found the strength to push up on the nails driven through his feet and with his last breath he said, "Father, into your hands I commit my spirit" (Luke 23:46). When it's out of your hands, put "it" in God's hands.

Reflection Journal: Are you ready for the help God is offering you? Will you put "it" in his hands? Why do you believe now is the time to let go of the anxiety crippling you?

_____

_____

_____

_____

_____

Fear Blocker

"Do not be anxious about anything, but in everything by prayer and supplication with thanksgiving let your request be made known to God. And the peace of God, which surpasses all understanding, will guard your hearts and mind in Christ Jesus" (Philippians 4:6–7 ESV).

■ ■ ■

Nothing Is Hopeless

THE ENEMY IS actively working to convince you your situation is hopeless. Today, trust that God is near you even if your apprehension is telling you the opposite. Hopelessness can become hopefulness once you realize God isn't in the business of letting you down. What you can't do, God can.

Key Verse: "When the righteous cry for help, the LORD hears and delivers them out of all their troubles. The LORD is near to the brokenhearted and saves the crushed in spirit" (Psalm 34:17–18 ESV).

I can't think of anything more hopeless than a crucifixion. Can you? No wonder the sun hid its face the day Jesus was beaten and nailed to the cross. Crucifixion is without a doubt, one of the cruelest and most humiliating forms of punishment and eventual death. The Romans were highly skilled in this art of execution. Nailed through the hands and feet, the victim was left to roast in the unrelenting desert sun. There was no escape. Birds of prey often perched on the cross beams, picking holes in the faces of the sufferers. Eventually, when all strength was gone and the victim could no longer push up for a breath, he died of suffocation. It's like drowning, while at the same time begging for water. I've worried about a lot of things in my life but being crucified has never crossed my mind.

It's hard to imagine the agony of being nailed to a cross. Once while building a house, I fell off a ladder onto a pile of old boards—one of which had a nail in it. The nail pierced my work boot and shot straight through the middle of my foot before exiting out the top. There aren't enough words in the English language to describe how much that hurt! All composure goes out the window when you have a nail through your foot. I can tell you without a doubt the embarrassment of screaming and hopping around like a lunatic was the last thing on my mind. Everyone at the job site knew something was wrong.

Make no mistake, the nails hurt Jesus too.

Jesus, our example, faced the same dilemma you and I face. Would he trust God's plan while suffering or would he spiral into despair? Even though Jesus knew about the promised resurrection, he had to refuse to surrender to the harassing thoughts of God not coming through for him. He had to wait, in the dark, as the plan of God came together.

Remember, when you trust in Christ, you are born into a kingdom where hope is always alive, and nothing is hopeless. The kingdom of heaven cannot be shaken by whatever is currently shaking you (Hebrews 12:28). When the Light of the world hung in darkness, the galleries of heaven remained well lit. Problems don't dim God's shine and they don't have to dim yours. John said it best in 1 John 1:5: "This is the message we have heard from him and declare to you; God is light; in him there is no darkness at all."

Reflection Journal: It's easy to spot what's going wrong in life but sometimes difficult to keep your eye on what's working in your favor. Jesus was promised a resurrection. What has God promised you?

_____

_____

_____

_____

_____

Fear Blocker

"Casting all your anxieties on him, because he cares for you" (1 Peter 5:7 ESV).

※ ※ ※

You'll Get Through This

REMEMBER—THIS IS not forever—it's just for now. You may have been temporarily set back but you can come back. No situation is beyond God's ability to repair. You can bounce higher than you fell.

Key Verse: "For as Jonah was three days and three nights in the belly of a huge fish, so the Son of Man will be three days and three nights in the heart of the earth" (Matthew 12:40).

While on the cross, Jesus knew something his problems were trying to get him to forget—tough times don't last. They buried him in a borrowed tomb because he wouldn't need it for long. Despairing times, for the believer, are short-lived. Like the tide, they momentarily wash over the shipwrecked carnage of our lives only to drift back out to sea. Jesus knew this. He had God's word on it! Months before the cross, he told the Pharisees what was going to happen. "Three days and I will be back on my feet!" Jesus declared. At the cross, Jesus had the opportunity to put his words into practice and to show the naysayers God doesn't walk out on his children. Jesus knew God had not brought him this far only to forget him and leave him in a mess. God births miracles; he doesn't abandon them.

When I was a boy, my dad was an avid raccoon hunter. In case you're not familiar with the sport, it is very popular in the

Ozark Hills of Missouri where I grew up. Using hounds, you trek through the woods at night hoping to scare a four-footed future Davy Crockett hat up a tree. When I was three years old, Dad took me on my first coon hunt. To make a long story short, he wasn't accustomed to me tagging along and in the excitement of the hunt, he forgot me in the woods! That's right—at three years old, I was left by myself in the dark. (Dad still feels bad about that one and I only remind him of it when I need a favor or a loan!)

Apparently, he didn't realize he left me until he arrived back home and Mom asked, "Where is Larry Joe?" In a wild panic they drove back to the woods and there I sat—right where he left me just a couple hours earlier. While earthly fathers are not perfect and sometimes forget, our heavenly Father will never forget. Even if your mind is telling you something different, your time in the dark is temporary. Don't worry, Daddy is on the way! Like the psalmist David said:

> God is our refuge and strength, an ever-present
> help in trouble. (Psalm 46:1)

Jesus also knew that what often looks like the end could be a new beginning in disguise.

Allow me to pose a question: What if what you see as a finish line is just the start of a whole new race? That's what it was for Jesus, and I have a sneaking suspicion God is up to more in your life than you think. The apostle Paul gives us a first-rate explanation of what really transpired at the cross:

> And being found in appearance as a man, he hum-
> bled himself and became obedient to death—even

death on a cross! Therefore, God exalted him to the
highest place and gave him the name that is above
every name. (Philippians 2:8–9)

Before the cross became a point of contention, Jesus had
already made a name for himself. Back-road beggars and rich
tax collectors knew him. Even the demons said, "[We] know
who you are" (Mark 1:24). However, his time in the dark only
elevated his status. Proving, your lowest place can be the vehicle
carrying you to your highest place! I am confident you would
stop stressing out over what you're currently not seeing if you
only knew what was coming! Before Jesus had a name above
every name, he had his name written on a cross (Matthew
27:37). A cross without a plan is something God would never
do. If you have a cross, God has a plan.

Jesus was well aware of the fact his destiny was on the other
side of his toughest challenge. His followers were often confused
only because they were looking at the cross with a "right now"
mentality. They could not fathom the amount of light waiting
just on the other side of the darkness. To them, the darkness
signified the end. To Jesus, the darkness was a doorway into his
brightest light and biggest fame.

Reflection Journal: As you confidently walk through this
season of difficulty, where do you see God taking you? How will
you be able to use what you've been through for God's glory?

_____

_____

Fear Blocker

"But seek first the kingdom of God and his righteousness, and all these things will be added to you. Therefore do not be anxious about tomorrow" (Matthew 6:33–34a ESV).

■ ■ ▨

Part I

Beacons of Light

- "The Life-Light blazed out of the darkness; the darkness couldn't put it out" (John 1:5 MSG).

- "I will lead the blind by ways they have not known, along unfamiliar paths I will guide them; I will turn the darkness into light before them and make the rough places smooth. These are the things I will do; I will not forsake them" (Isaiah 42:16).

- "People sitting out their lives in the dark saw a huge light; sitting in the dark, dark country of death they watched the sun come up" (Matthew 4:16 MSG).

A Story of Unshakable Faith

Veronica and her family were vacationing in Florida. Disney seemed the perfect place to take four young daughters. What could possibly go wrong at the happiest place on earth? Bella, her third child, is proof how in an instant the brightest day can turn into the darkest night. Veronica sat poolside at the resort when the lifeguard blew the whistle. The scene became chaotic. Adults jumped in the deep end as frightened children hurried to their parents. Someone in the water was in trouble. "My girls were right in front of me or so I thought. I remember finding it peculiar that the little girl they were pulling out of the deep water was wearing the same bathing suit as my Bella," Veronica said.

At once, reality set in. It was Bella. Apparently, she slipped past Veronica and was trying to swim to her older sister when she sank to the bottom of the pool.

Four-year-old Bella was a grayish purple when they pulled her out of the water and she wasn't breathing. By the time the ambulance arrived, her lips were blue. Bella hadn't taken a breath in ten minutes . . .

Veronica's voice cracked as she explained what happened next. "On the way to the hospital I called my pastor. We prayed over Bella and asked God for a miracle. It was completely out of our hands now. That is when it happened. Bella gasped for a breath; then another, and another! By the time we arrived at the hospital, she was breathing completely on her own," she said. After a thorough exam, Bella was released the same day. She is now a teenager and in perfect health.

In the dark, Veronica had a choice to make. She could have accepted what was happening and give up but instead she decided to believe God for a miracle. Veronica went on to say,

"Just because 'it's' drowned, doesn't mean 'it's' dead. I trusted God when what I feared the most happened, and others should do the same when they find themselves in a similar situation, because you never know what God is about to do."

PART II
YOU'LL NEVER BE LEFT
IN THE GRAVE

*They found the stone rolled away from
the tomb, but when they entered they did not
find the body of the Lord Jesus. While they were
wondering about this, suddenly two men in
clothes that gleamed like lightning stood beside
them. In their fright the women bowed down
with their faces to the ground, but the men said
to them, "Why do you look for the living among
the dead? He is not here; he has risen!*
(Luke 24:2–6a)

Good things fall apart so better things can fall together.

The Grave Can't Hold You

PRETENDING EVERYTHING IS alright seldom has benefit. The "grave" may still have your attention but it's not your destination. Even Jesus was "laid" in darkness. The grave situation, however, could not hold him and it cannot hold you.

Key Verse: "The women who had come with Jesus from Galilee followed Joseph and saw the tomb and how his body was laid in it" (Luke 23:55).

"How are you?"

"Fine."

If by "fine" you mean broken, depressed, screaming, giving up, tortured, alienated, and bruised, then I guess you're fine. This, no doubt, is how the followers of Jesus felt the day they buried their faithful Master. When the thing you loved and pinned the future on is dead, you're not fine. You more likely feel agitation and apprehension.

Like the women in this story, are you still looking at a tomb? Do you see a lifeless body where once stood what you thought was your hope? Did something you thought would always be alive, suddenly die? Maybe the death happened to your marriage, a career, a valued relationship, ministry, dream, or even someone you loved dearly. The women came to view what they lost. Are you still viewing what you've lost and have you decided life can never be good again because of what you've been though?

When something you love dies, you can die with it or you can look ahead to a guaranteed resurrection that may or may not look anything like you thought. Solomon said the grave is never satisfied. It never says, I have enough (Proverbs 30:16). The grave will not easily give you up. The grave craves fresh victims. New arrivals are closely watched and conditioned to stay. The grave knows it's easier for you to lie down in a six-foot hole than it is to stand up and face your fears with the confident assurance everything is going to be okay.

On at least three occasions, Jesus told his disciples he was going to die. He also promised them he would rise again. His death came with a guarantee. He was saying, "It may look like it's over but it's far from over. You don't have to be anxious. I guarantee it." Losing something you hoped to keep forever can be devastating. You can even feel as if life will never be good again. The fact you hurt so deeply only proves what you lost mattered to you. When you're trapped in a grave of uncertainty, you must remember Jesus is a grave robber. Don't pick out your tombstone just yet. Focus on the words of the prophet:

> "For I know the plans I have for you," declares the LORD, "plans to prosper you and not to harm you, plans to give you a hope and a future." (Jeremiah 29:11)

What the disciples thought they were losing forever was actually just the plan of God shifting away from what they thought was going to happen. God doesn't need your permission to flip the script in life. He does, however, desire your partnership.

Reflection Journal: God didn't create you to feel dead inside. Today, pour out your feelings. Don't "fancy" it up or tell God what you think he wants to hear. Be honest with him and share exactly what's bothering you. Plead your case.

Fear Blocker

"I can do all things through him who strengthens me" (Philippians 4:13 ESV).

■ ▨ ▨

Something Better Is on the Way

WHEN JESUS WAS resurrected, he didn't pretend he was never crucified. He wasn't going to pick up where he left off and continue as if nothing traumatic happened. Jesus had scars and so will you. I know this may sound alarming but it's good news.

Key Verse: "While they were still talking about this, Jesus himself stood among them, 'Peace be with you.' They were startled and frightened, thinking they saw a ghost. He said to them, 'Why are you troubled, and why do doubts rise in your minds? Look at my hands and my feet. It is I myself! Touch me and see; a ghost does not have flesh and bones, as you see I have'" (Luke 24:36–39).

The scars marking the body of Jesus were telltale signs of the trauma he experienced. Scars on his hands for all the things you should have never touched. Scars on his brow for all the thoughts you should have never had. Scars on his feet for all the places you should have never walked. Scars on his side to release all the poison you have spewed onto others. Scars on his back for the times you turned your back on him. Like you, Jesus was unfairly marked by what he went through. These marks or scars could have easily defined Jesus's identity. He could have been known as the man whipped by others, instead of being known as the man who whipped death, hell, and the grave. In the same way, your "marks" often decide what kind of mark you will leave. In the middle of your distress, when life is spinning out of control, will you be known as a conqueror or as the one who was conquered?

As was the case with the disciples, when something good in your life dies, God is not going to resurrect something completely foreign to you. God knows your taste. He knows what you like and what brings you happiness. God didn't resurrect a stranger and present him as a new Master to the disciples. No, God resurrected the familiar. When Jesus rose from the grave, he was still Jesus—only new and improved. His time in the dark actually energized his life and enhanced the person he already was.

During worrisome times, you can become hysterical, thinking the life you loved is forever lost. Like the disciples, you can get scared and start telling ghost stories. Panicked, you might believe what was taken can never again be regained. Keep in mind, after he was crucified, Jesus was still very much Jesus. He looked like Jesus. He laughed like Jesus. He even cooked fish like Jesus (John 21:9). The difference was, he now had power over death. The disciples freaked out when he died but the truth was, life for them would be enhanced because of his death. What he was willing to go through was part of their breakthrough.

During seasons of uncertainty, you don't have to be nervous about the outcome. While what you lost will always be part of you, God is working on a new set of blueprints. Just like the stone blocked the entrance of the tomb, eclipsing the resurrection, you may not be able to see what God is doing with what is dead. Let me assure you, he is paving the road to a place called "happy." You can trust him.

Reflection Journal: Scars are healed marks and proof of what you've successfully been through. Like Jesus, examine your scars today. What do they tell you about the future?

Fear Blocker

"Cast your cares on the LORD, and he will sustain you; he will never let the righteous be shaken" (Psalm 55:22 ESV).

You're Not Buried, You're Planted

THE DOOR LEADING you into better days can be shrouded in uncertainty. The path forward doesn't always look like the way out. The weight of all you've been under may still feel particularly crushing. Keep going!

Key Verse: "Don't, enemy, crow over me. I'm down, but I'm not out. I'm sitting in the dark right now, but God is my light" (Micah 7:8 MSG).

I really believe the above verse is what Jesus was thinking as he approached death on the cross—the setback was paving the way for the greatest comeback of all time. God would get him through more than just the actual crucifixion. He would also get Jesus through the following days. God knows your struggle is so much bigger than just a one-day event. God will never say to you, "You should be over this by now." He will, however, say, "Let me help you get over what has been dragging you under."

Having spent thousands of hours as a professional counselor, I know the aftermath of the crisis can be far worse than the event. The downward spiral of emotions can last for an indefinite period and become all-consuming. You panic when the lights initially go out but you fall apart when you realize

they aren't going to immediately come back on. Don't forget
God was with Jesus in every stage of his dilemma. He was there
before they drove the nails through his hands and feet and he
stuck around after those nails were removed so his lifeless body
could be washed and placed in the tomb. Others may have
walked out on you but God won't. Leaving is not in his nature.
David said it best:

> Therefore, my heart is glad and my tongue rejoices;
> my body also will rest secure, because you will not
> abandon me to the realm of the dead, nor will you
> let your faithful one see decay. You make known to
> me the path of life; you will fill me with joy in your
> presence, with eternal pleasures at your right hand.
> (Psalm 16:9–11)

When you feel abandoned and unsettled, you can rejoice
and be glad. Jesus said, "Unless a kernel of wheat falls to the
ground and dies, it remains only a single seed. But if it dies, it
produces many seeds" (John 12:24). During seasons of uncertainty, you don't have to be nervous about the outcome. While
what you lost will always be part of you, God is working on a
new set of blueprints. Just like the stone blocked the entrance
of the tomb, eclipsing the resurrection, you may not be able to
see what God is doing with what is dead. Let me assure you, he
is paving the road to a place called "happy." You can trust him.
    What if you saw yourself as being planted instead being
buried? Would that calm your emotions?
    In my mind, I can see a little seed. He has just been pack-
aged and is excited to be shipped out to his new home. When
he arrives at his destination, the sower takes him out of the

safety of the bag and places him in the cold, dark ground. The seed is thinking to himself, *This is not what I signed up for. I thought I was going to become that beautiful flower on the box I was shipped in. No one told me it was going to be so dark and lonely here. I was lied to. It's over for me.* Once in the ground, something unexpected begins to happen. A green shoot breaks through his hull and like two hands, begin reaching upward. Soon he bursts through the dirt and experiences his first taste of sunshine. It isn't long until the little seed realizes what was happening all along. The dark ground prepared the way for him to become the picture of the beautiful flower on the box. He wasn't buried in a grave; he was planted in a bed!

What if the grave you think you're in is actually a seedbed of miracles? God is not a coroner. He is a gardener! The cave of tension you're experiencing is not your final resting place. You can grow through what you go through!

Reflection Journal: Make a list of all the ways God is growing you. How will you use what he is teaching you to get through the aftermath?

Fear Blocker

"Have I not commanded you? Be strong and courageous. Do not be afraid; do not be discouraged, for the Lord your God will be with you wherever you go" (Joshua 1:9).

■ ■ ■

Part II

Beacons of Light

- "Do this and the lights will turn on, and your lives will turn around at once. Your righteousness will pave your way. The God of glory will secure your passage. Then when you pray, God will answer. You'll call out for help and I'll say, 'Here I am'" (Isaiah 58:8–9 MSG).

- "You groped your way through that murk once, but no longer. You're out in the open now. The bright light of Christ makes your way plain. So no more stumbling around. Get on with it!" (Ephesians 5:10 MSG).

- "What came into existence was Life, and the Life was Light to live by. The Life-Light blazed out of the darkness; the darkness couldn't put it out" (John 1:4–5 MSG).

A Story of Unshakable Faith

Danny and Jenny had a fairytale wedding. On Valentine's Day, they exchanged vows in front of 500 friends and family members. She wore a full-length, hand-tailored, white wedding dress, and he, the same Marine uniform he wore the day he proposed. Over the next five years, God blessed the family with three children: Danny Jr., Hannah, and Ethan. Then Jenny was pregnant with baby number four.

On Sunday December 14, 1997, life forever changed for the White family. Having been reassigned to Fort Leonard Wood in Missouri, they packed up and hit the road. After stopping for breakfast in Arizona, Danny buckled in the kids. Five-year-old Danny Jr. and nine-month-old Ethan rode with Jenny, while three-year-old Hannah rode with her dad in a second vehicle. After a day of travel, Danny glanced in his rearview mirror and was horrified to see Jenny's Ford Explorer go off the road and begin flipping like a corkscrew. To this day, no one knows why.

Tragically, Jenny, her unborn child, and Danny Jr. all lost their lives in the accident. Danny said, "I felt waves of helplessness and hopelessness wash over me as I stood at mile marker 31.9 on I-40 East, outside Kingman, Arizona. I felt alone and forsaken by God." Danny learned firsthand, how life can blackout in an instant. But instead of turning away from God, he chose to turn toward God. Later, he met and married Nora. Together they had six more children and Nora adopted Hannah and Ethan.

After retiring from the Marine Corps as a Lieutenant Colonel, Danny founded *Lead with Liberty*. This ministry offers hope and encouragement to tired, thirsty souls. The devastation of his past is now a beacon of hope to those who feel lost in life's desert. (For the full story, read *The Widower's Walk* by Danny White.)

I think it's important for me to add one more piece of information. As I listened to Danny recount the events of his story, something leaped inside of me when he mentioned the exact location where he stood helpless and stunned, the day of the accident. He stood at mile marker 31.9 and I immediately thought of a Scripture:

> Be merciful to me, LORD, for I am in distress; my eyes grow weak with sorrow, and my soul and body with grief. (Psalm 31:9)

It was no accident Danny was standing at mile marker 31.9. As I shared this verse with him, he began to weep, as once again God proved himself faithful.

PART III
IT IS FINISHED, BUT YOU ARE NOT FINISHED

When he had received the drink, Jesus said, "It is finished." With that, he bowed his head and gave up his spirit. (John 19:30)

"Hope is being able to see that there is light despite all of the darkness." —Desmond Tutu

It's a Comma, Not a Period

JUST BECAUSE YOU turn a page, doesn't mean you finished a chapter. God is the author and finisher of your faith. Trust his pen as he writes your story. You don't have to be nervous about the ending or worry about a cliff-hanger moment that never gets resolved. Soon you will see the big picture and realize your best days are still to come.

Key Verse: "Looking unto Jesus the author and finisher of our faith; who for the joy that was set before him endured the cross, despising the shame, and is set down at the right hand of the throne of God" (Hebrews 12:2 kjv).

If God is an author, then your life is a book in progress. And like a good book, sometimes a chapter will end before you are ready. The page turns but you're still stuck somewhere in the backstory. You weren't ready for it to be finished. After all, you fell in love with the characters, plot, and descriptions. Now the author has moved on or perhaps even completed the series, you feel cheated. You think to yourself, *It can't be over. I am not emotionally prepared for this!* Finishing an intriguing story is one thing—feeling finished in life is another.

I'm sure the followers of Jesus felt that way the day he died. Had God really placed a period where they thought would be a comma? Was it really finished? The story was over before the climax. When life isn't making sense, it can feel like the author has put down his pen prematurely. Jesus was dead, along with their hopes and dreams. In their minds, there were no more chapters to be written. As far as they were concerned, they finished the book and were staring at a big, bold THE END.

God is a loving Father. Even when life takes a turn for the worse, he always has your back and he will never leave your side. Your present trouble does not indicate his absence. Your struggle is not God's fault, nor did he cause your predicament. In fact, if you're going to get through this stressful time, you will need his help now more than ever. God understands your skepticism. He knows how frightened you are and how weak you feel. He is not asking you to hold onto him. Rather, he is requesting permission to hold onto you:

> Take my side as you promised; I'll live then for sure. Don't disappoint all my grand hopes. Stick with me and I'll be alright. (Psalm 119:116 MSG)

The above verse piques my interest. It contradicts the advice I have received from well-meaning Christians over the years. During a period of pain, David never said, "Lord, I am on your side! I won't disappoint you! I am sticking with you until the end!" Rather, he said, "Lord, take my side, don't disappoint me, and stick with me." David was no pretender. He wasn't trying to work up a spiritual high or impress God with religious talking points. He was just being honest about how his life felt at the moment and wasn't trying to hide his feelings of doubt.

Like David, you can say, "God please hold onto me, because I am having trouble holding onto you." God isn't moved by spiritual hype. He prefers brutal honesty. Putting on your Sunday best, going to church, and pretending to be okay isn't nearly as effective as putting aside your pride, going to God, and admitting you're not okay.

Reflection Journal: Do you feel like God stopped writing your life story mid-sentence? Hold on to him as he finishes that sentence and make it your prayer today.

Fear Blocker

"When anxiety was great within me, your consolation brought me joy" (Psalm 94:19).

▨ ▨ ▨

Bruised but Not Broken

JESUS WAS A bruised, bloody mess—not a broken mess. The enemy never broke him. Today, stand tall.

Key Verse: "But when they came to Jesus and found that he was already dead, they did not break his legs" (John 19:33).

The soldiers never broke the legs of Jesus, and your current situation doesn't have the power to break you. His bruises weren't a sign of weakness. They signaled he could take punch after punch and keep going (John 19:3). You're much stronger than you think. Your broken heart doesn't have to translate into a broken life. The psalmist declared:

> The LORD is close to the brokenhearted and saves those who are crushed in spirit. The righteous person may have many troubles, but the Lord delivers him from them all; he protects all his bones, not one of them will be broken. (Psalm 34:18–20)

God travels broken roads looking for those crushed in spirit. Wounded hearts on winding backstreets call to him. He cannot stay away. Like a storm chaser, he runs into your tornado. It's our broken hearts and crushed spirits he can't resist.

In the above verse, *broken* is the Hebrew word *shavar*. It means: to break into pieces, shatter, crush, demolish, smash, and be shipwrecked. *Crushed* is the Hebrew word *dakka*. It means: bruised, destroyed, and feeling like you are in a grave with the weight of the world upon you. When the adjectives describing your bruised life are piling up, God says, "I am close."

Interestingly enough, the Hebrew word for *close* is *qarov*. It means near and physical closeness between people, such as family members. This same word is also used in Deuteronomy 4:7 describing God's relationship with the nation of Israel.

When our spirits are crushed and brokenness sets in, we often believe that is when God is the farthest away. In our minds, we think if God were close, we wouldn't feel so lost in the dark. However, according to the word, this is when God is actually the closest! That is why you can be bruised but not broken. Paul writes:

> We've been surrounded and battered by troubles, but we're not demoralized; we're not sure what to do, but we know that God knows what to do; we've been spiritually terrorized, but God hasn't left our side; we've been thrown down, but we haven't broken. What they did to Jesus, they do to us—trial and torture, mockery and murder; what Jesus did among them, he does in us—he lives! Our lives are at constant risk for Jesus' sake, which makes Jesus' life all the more evident in us. While we're going through the worst, you're getting in on the best! We're not keeping this quiet, not on your life. (2 Corinthians 4:8–13 MSG)

Life may have thrown Paul down but he believed God would raise him. The crucifixion of Jesus taught him he can stand tall when his legs aren't broken! What if you stood wobbly-legged in the dark and believed what you used to only proclaim in the light? What if you allow your wound to be the place where the light enters you?

Reflection Journal: You've proven you can take a punch. How will you punch back?

Fear Blocker

"When I am afraid, I put my trust in you" (Psalm 56:3).

⬛ ⬛ ⬛

Don't Be Troubled

JESUS KNEW A storm was brewing. He could see the dark clouds rolling in. Troubling times were ahead but he wasn't troubled. Jesus had a quiet confidence and he refused to allow his mind to dwell on the difficulty he was facing. Today, challenge every troubling thought.

Key Verse: "Do not let your hearts be troubled. You believe in God; believe also in me. My Father's house has many rooms; if that were not so, would I have told you that I am going there to prepare a place for you?" (John 14:1–2).

Right before Jesus declared this famous passage, he predicted Peter's denial:

> Then Jesus answered, "Will you really lay down your life for me? Very truly I tell you, before the rooster crows, you will disown me three times!" (John 13:38)

Jesus didn't say, "All right, everyone has a future except for Peter. He is going to deny me." No, Jesus included Peter in the future plan, even though he was shaky in his faith. Jesus has also included you regardless how unstable you feel at the moment. The crowing rooster wasn't meant to signal Peter's faithlessness, it was meant to declare Jesus's faithfulness. Having been raised on a farm, I know from personal experience roosters crow while it's still dark. They aren't announcing the darkness; they are declaring the light. The crowing rooster proved to Peter, Jesus would not forget him even though Peter would deny him. Even the angels who appeared at the tomb of Jesus were in on how much Jesus loved and cared for Peter. Listen to what they said:

> "Don't be alarmed," he said. "You are looking for Jesus the Nazarene, who was crucified. He has risen! He is not here. See the place where they laid him. But go, tell his disciples and Peter, 'He is going ahead of you into Galilee. There you will see him, just as he told you.'" (Mark 16:6–7)

The angel mentions Peter by name. The question is, why? I have always heard preachers say it was because Peter lost his discipleship when he denied Jesus; therefore, Jesus excluded him from the twelve. However, that is not what I see in this story. I have a feeling Peter was more than distraught over his denial of the Master—regretting and replaying his horrifying actions. I think the angel mentioned Peter to calm his nerves, even though Peter had made a terrible choice during an anxious moment. He wanted Peter to know what he said while feeling overwhelmed would not be held against him. The plan of God wasn't canceled just because in a moment of weakness Peter reverted back to the man he was before Jesus found him. The angel said Peter's name to remind him Jesus hadn't forgotten it.

During life's darkest days, we tend to say and do things that do not represent the true intentions of our hearts. Like Peter, when the future is stripped, whipped, and standing naked in front of us, we often forget God has a resurrection planned. I am thankful God doesn't hold our human weakness against us. If my relationship with God was based upon how perfect my actions are when I'm hurting, I would be in real trouble. This portion is not an excuse to lose your mind when your anxiety level rises. It only serves to remind you your mistakes and misgivings about what God is and isn't allowing in your life, does not change what God is preparing for you. God created you and knows you'll occasionally struggle to keep it together.

The crowing rooster wasn't an end-all; it was a wakeup call. Thank goodness God looks out for us when our outlook overlooks him!

Reflection Journal: Like Peter, are you acting in ways that contradict your normal behavior. How will you change this?

_____

_____

_____

_____

Fear Blocker

"Trust in the LORD with all your heart and lean not on your own understanding; in all your ways submit to him, and he will make your paths straight" (Proverbs 3:5–6).

Part III

Beacons of Light

- "By your words I can see where I'm going; they throw a beam of light on my dark path" (Psalm 119:105 MSG).

- "He energizes those who get tired, gives fresh strength to dropouts" (Isaiah 40:29 MSG).

- "Break open your words, let the light shine out, let ordinary people see the meaning" (Psalm 119:130 MSG).

A Story of Unshakable Faith

Jana thought her life with Bill would have a happy ending. They had five children and she was pregnant with baby number six. She worked at a job she loved and they lived in a nice house. Jana thought the adventure was just beginning—until life tried to tell her she was finished. "It all began to unravel," she said. "I found out that Bill had been having an affair for some time. To top it off, he also confessed to a drug addiction." Bill was unwilling to leave his mistress, and saw his drug use as Jana's problem. So, she packed up their five children, loaded as much as she could in the family car, and drove halfway across the country to live with her parents.

Listen to Jana in her own words as she describes her emotional despair. "For the first time in my life, I felt immobilized, confused, and completely lost. God had given me so much, and at the time, I felt like he was the one taking it away. I did not understand. If I truly was a part of God's family, why would he allow this to happen to my family?"

Jana, like so many, understandably went down the road of self-pity. She blamed God, her husband, and his drug use for her overwhelming anxiety. To make matters worse, in the midst of the confusion, she allowed herself to become a lukewarm Christian. At the bottom, in the dark, is where Jana began to once again seek the light only God can bring. Jana went on to say, "When you have everything you think you need—you can push out the One you need the most. I didn't know if my husband and I would be able to restore our marriage, but I did start believing that God had a future for me and our children, regardless." Jana began cleansing her life of what she described as negative noise. She rejected unhealthy television, radio, and social media outlets. She began focusing her mind on God and how he wanted to rebuild her life. She said, "Even though my marriage to Bill was never restored, I wasn't finished because God wasn't finished!"

Jana continued to work on her faith by developing a closer and more meaningful relationship with Christ. She also focused her attention on being a good example for her children. As a result, she not only found a deeper connection with God but also a more fulfilling life than the one she thought was unfairly ripped away.

PART IV
STAY OUT OF THE GRAVEYARD

They were puzzled, wondering what to make of this. Then, out of nowhere it seemed, two men, light cascading over them, stood there. The women were awestruck and bowed down in worship. The men said, "Why are you looking for the Living One in a cemetery?" (Luke 24:4–5 MSG)

"Let your hopes, not your hurts, shape your future." —Robert Schuller

God Is Likely to Use the Unlikely

WHEN NOTHING IS making sense, God is likely to do something that will leave you scratching your head. He will even use the absurd and unbelievable to carry you. Today, watch for Joseph.

Key Verse: "Now there was a man named Joseph, a member of the Council, a good and upright man, who had not consented to their decision and action. He came from the Judean town of Arimathea and he was waiting for the kingdom of God. Going to Pilate, he asked for Jesus' body. Then he took it down, wrapped it in linen cloth and placed it in a tomb cut in the rock, one in which no one had yet been laid" (Luke 23:50–53).

In ancient times, the remains of an executed criminal were often left unburied or at best placed in a pauper's field. A near relative, such as a parent, might be given the body, but even that was highly unlikely. In the case of Jesus, something very unusual happened. The body of Jesus was given to a member of the Sanhedrin. The Sanhedrin was a religious council of men who acted as judges in Israel and had full authority over the people. Joseph was a part of this group and apparently was absent the day they demanded Jesus be crucified, for he had not consented to their decision (Mark 14:64).

We have no record of anyone other than Joseph requesting to carry the body of Jesus. There were obviously many other more likely candidates. What about all the people Jesus healed, fed, and delivered from demons? Where were they and what about Lazarus? He of all people owed Jesus a mountain-sized debt. The woman at the well and the woman caught in adultery might not have been able to lug his body on their own but they could have partnered in carrying him. All were no-shows. God used the most unimaginable character to bear the body of his Son and he will do the same for you.

When you're racked with worry, look for Joseph. Look for the unordinary ways God has prearranged to pick you up. Look for the unlikely. Your pallbearer may seem a bit out of place.

I am convinced you can miss God's answer to your crisis, simply because it doesn't fit your preconceived notion of how God should help you overcome your trouble. God doesn't need your nod of approval. He needs your full cooperation. The psalmist David, explained it this way in Psalm 139:12 (MSG): "It's a fact: darkness isn't dark to you; night and day, darkness and night, they're all the same to you."

If God can use a member of the Sanhedrin to carry his Son during his biggest challenge—he can also use the implausible people, places, and things in your life to carry you when you can't take another step on your own. We are conditioned to seek the predictable in times of crisis. God is not predictable. He is so much more than stained glass. He is creative, wild, and free to do as he wishes.

Reflection Journal: Now would be a good time to place a book-mark, find a quiet place, and consider the unlikely ways God has been revealing himself all along. Come back later and write down all your "Joseph" moments.

_____

_____

_____

_____

Fear Blocker

"I lift my eyes to the mountains—where does my help come from? My help comes from the LORD, the Maker of heaven and earth. He will not let your foot slip—he who watches over you will not slumber; indeed, he who watches over Israel will neither slumber nor sleep. The LORD watches over you—the LORD is your shade at your right hand; the sun will not harm you by day, nor the moon at night. The LORD will keep you from all harm—he will watch over your life; the LORD will watch over your coming and going both now and forevermore" (Psalm 121:1–8).

█ █ █

Don't Look for the Living Among the Dead

REFUSE TO HANG out in the dead places of your past. Remember—the tunnel of darkness is actually a birthing canal—leading you into a new life. What you fear has no power other than what you provide.

Key Verse: "Why are you looking for the Living One in a cemetery?" (Luke 24:5b MSG).

Old cemeteries dot the landscape around the tiny town of Hartville, Missouri, where I grew up. Having been both a Civil War battle site (The Battle of Hartville, 1863) and home to several Native American tribes, old graves are not hard to find. On more than one occasion, I have found myself walking through an overgrown graveyard. Names carved in rock spark my imagination. Who were they? What did they look like? How did they die? How did they get here? I will never know. None are alive to tell me their story. Death has silenced them. In all my exploring, I have never encountered the living among the dead—and neither will you.

After Joseph carried the body of Jesus to the cemetery, we have no record of him ever returning. There was, however, a group of women who came to the graveyard the morning of the resurrection. Luke points out the purpose of this visit: "Then they went home and prepared spices and perfumes" (Luke 23:56a).

Their intentions were good. After all, they just wanted to honor Jesus by anointing his body with oils and perfumes, but upon arrival they were met by two angels. Appearing as shafts of light, in an otherwise dark situation, the angels asked the women why they came. This was an odd question. After all, the women were there when Jesus died (Luke 23:49). They felt the darkness gripping the earth as he took his last breath. I can see them huddled together, holding hands, as the ground under their feet shook in protest. The once majestic Christ was reduced to a corpse right in front of them. Now they were being questioned as to why they came to his tomb. Of course, they were in the graveyard! Where else would they be?

The angels had to remind them of what Jesus promised:

> "He is not here; he has risen! Remember how he told you, while he was still with you in Galilee: 'The Son of man must be delivered into the hands of sinful men, be crucified and on the third day be raised again.'" Then they remembered his words. (Luke 24:6–8)

Jesus would sleep three days, rise, and shine! It was the morning of the third day. Jesus was up by now. They were more likely to find him at Dunkin Donuts than a cemetery!

Overwhelmed by trouble and grief, these women had no expectation of resurrection. Even though Jesus demonstrated his power to them over and over, they were still unable to believe he would live again.

There is a valuable lesson here—one we often overlook. At some point, if you're going to live an unshakable life, you have to stop anointing what is dead. You must refuse to make that familiar trip to the graveyard you made so many times before. Reliving the hell you went through will only keep you trapped in the tragedies of yesterday. The angels were right. You're never going to find the living among the dead. That statement was true then—and it's true now.

If you're going to anoint something, anoint the future! Throw your bag of burial spices heavenward and watch as they fall onto a path leading to a new day. The perfume you were saving to cover the smell of death, can be poured out before God in an act of worship!

Reflection Journal: How will you stay out of the graveyard of despair? What changes do you need to make in your daily routine?

Fear Blocker

"No, in all things we are more than conquerors through him who loved us. For I am convinced that neither death nor life, neither angels nor demons, neither present nor the future, nor any power, neither height nor depth, nor anything else in all creation, will be able to separate us from the love of God that is in Christ Jesus our Lord" (Romans 8:37–39).

※ ※ ※

Overcoming a Wide-Awake Nightmare

JOB, LIKE JESUS, learned firsthand how life can go from good to bad and without any forewarning. Today, is a turn-around day.

Key Verse: "The LORD blessed the latter part of Job's life more than the first" (Job 42:12).

If there is one person in the Scriptures, other than Jesus, who lived a nightmare, it was Job of the Old Testament. If problems were paychecks, he would have been a multimillionaire. Large family gatherings and green fields full of the best livestock were replaced by caskets and catastrophe. In a very short amount of time, Job lost everything dear to him, including his children. He went from wealthy farmer to flat-broke gravedigger in a single day. Job wasn't shy about telling God how he felt during his ordeal:

> "Instead of bread I get groans for my supper, then leave the table and vomit my anguish. The worst of my fears has come true, what I've dreaded most has happened. My repose is shattered, my peace

destroyed. No rest for me, ever—death has invaded
life." (Job 3:24–26 msg)

When life went off the cliff of despair, like so many, Job ran a
gamut of emotions. In a moment of weakness and desperation,
he even blamed God for his trouble, declaring God was the one
who yanked hope out by the roots (Job 19:10). Of course, we
know the real culprit was the devil. Satan thought once trouble
came, Job would forget about God and all the days of lavish
blessing. As a result, death invaded the farm and took hostages.
Job was completely crushed under the canopy of darkness. He
felt like he was trapped in an endless night (Job 7:3).

Job's story demonstrates you can be both wide awake
and experiencing a nightmare at the same time. Job's worst
nightmares never involved sleep. After he lost everything, Job
approached God with an interesting question:

> "Where's the strength to keep my hopes up? What
> future do I have to keep me going?" (Job 6:11 msg)

Job's question deserved to be answered. He was in the middle
of a catastrophe. Maybe you've asked God that same question.
I have. It's when you say, "What's the deal, God? Are you dou-
ble-crossing me? You promised a future, but I can't see it."

During his crisis Job is visited by a group of friends. They
weren't much help but one in particular catches my attention.
His name is Zophar. He tells Job the reason his life is falling
apart is because of sin. He even wishes God would give Job a
piece of his mind and show him why the darkness is his fault
(Job 11:3). We all know a Zophar or two. Listen as he prophe-
sies to Job without realizing what he is saying:

"You will surely forget your trouble, recalling it only as waters gone by. Life will be brighter than noonday, and darkness will become like morning. You will be secure, because there is hope; you will look about you and take rest in safety. You will lie down, with no one to make you afraid, and many will court your favor." (Job 11:16–19)

What a great word!

The end of Job's story and the end of yours can be the same. God can bless you with more than you lost. God still gives double for your trouble!

Reflection Journal: What does the future you're praying for look like? Be specific.

_____

_____

_____

_____

_____

Fear Blocker

"At this, Job got up and tore his robe and shaved his head. Then he fell to the ground in worship and said: 'Naked I came from the mother's womb, and naked I will depart. The LORD gave and the LORD has taken away; may the name of the LORD be praised.'

In all this, Job did not sin by charging God with wrongdoing"
(Job 1:20–22).

▓ ▒ ▒

Part IV

Beacons of Light

- "This in essence, is the message we heard from Christ and
  are passing on to you; God is light, pure light; there's not a
  trace of darkness in him. If we claim that we experience a
  shared life with him and continue to stumble around in the
  dark, we're obviously lying through our teeth—we are not
  living what we claim" (1 John 1:5–6 MSG).

- "No, despite all these things, overwhelming victory is ours
  though Christ, who loved us" (Romans 8:37 NLT).

- "Your sun shall no more go down, nor your moon withdraw
  itself; for the LORD will be your everlasting light, and your
  days of mourning shall be ended" (Isaiah 60:20 ESV).

A Story of Unshakable Faith

Becky and Steve fell in love, got married, and began life
together in small town America. God blessed their union with
two children. Soon they found themselves working side by side
at the same job. Life was going as planned and without much
complication.

Steve had the day off. Becky had to work. When she arrived
that morning, her cell phone rang. She was unable to take the
call and didn't recognize the number anyway. Later, she called

back and that is when panic set in. The number belonged to the local coroner's office. The only thing they would tell her over the phone was the police were on their way to talk to her. In hysteria, she called the school and to her relief, both of the children were safe. Becky then called Steve but there was no answer. She tried calling again and again—still no answer. Then the police arrived and she was brought into her boss's office. "Steve was killed this morning," they said. "He was hit head-on not far from where you live. We're sorry."

Becky described the moments to follow. "I felt devastated. Like a balloon slowly losing air, all the wind was knocked out of me. Was this really happening? It was a nightmare that I couldn't wake up from." Over the next few months, the circumstances surrounding Steve's death played over and over in her mind on a continuous loop. She was angry and stuck. *What could I have done differently and why did it happen?* she thought.

Instead of living in the current moment, she was reliving the events of that awful day. The calendar changed but her season of pain didn't. Something had to give and fast. For the sake of her children and her own sanity, Becky soon realized even though she would never fully get over Steve's death, she had to put it behind her and move on. "Things began to change for me when I started talking about the good times we shared, rather than talking about the day of the accident. Instead of being angry over time lost with Steve, I began to be thankful for time shared with him. This required a complete reversal in my behavior. I am not going to lie, it was not easy, but I realized that even though life would never be like it once was, it could be good again."

I think it's worth noting at the time of this interview nine years have passed. Becky left me with these words. "I am still not completely over it and probably won't ever be, but I am no longer revisiting the past and the pain of what happened. My kids turned out great and they like to watch home movies of their dad. I've learned that life doesn't always go as planned, and I am now looking forward to the future, even though it's not what I originally thought it would be." When Becky decided to no longer allow her past pain to decide her current happiness, life changed for the better. She offers additional proof the angel at the tomb was correct. You'll never find the living among the dead.

PART V
YOU ARE NOT FORSAKEN

And at three in the afternoon Jesus cried out in a loud voice, "Eloi, Eloi, lama sabachthani?" (which means, "My God, my God, why have you forsaken me?"). (Mark 15:34)

"Every time that you feel abandoned, every time you feel alone, Jesus is near."
—Anonymous

God Can See You When You Can't See Him

REGARDLESS WHAT YOUR feelings are telling you, dare to believe God has his eyes on you, even if you're unable to put your eyes on him.

Key Verse: "Then I said to myself, 'Oh, he even sees me in the dark! At night I'm immersed in the light'" (Psalm 139:11 MSG).

At noon, the day Jesus was crucified, the sky became black and ominous. Thick darkness rolled in as daylight rolled out. Jesus groaned in misery as the depths of his suffering took him deeper into the shadows. In agony, he looked heavenward and shouted, "Why have you turned away from me? Where are you? Can't you see how abandoned I feel?" He was hurting and scared. He needed a hand to hold.

In a state of limbo, Jesus felt abandoned by God. Past blessings and future promises are hard to see when you feel all alone. Jesus was having difficulty keeping his emotions together when he found himself suspended between what was and what will be. The weight of what he was going through was heavy and beginning to take its toll on his state of mind. He was sinking under the load and at his breaking point. Does that sound familiar? In this weakened condition, Jesus questioned God concerning his seeming absence. Had God really brought Jesus this far only to leave him to face the cross by himself? A better question might be, would God walk out on you while darkness is running in?

Remember, Jesus was still flesh and bones at this point. While he was sinless, he wasn't exempt from human emotions and the unsettling thought of not knowing exactly how everything would play out. Fear and panic aren't impressed with your Christian credentials. Despair doesn't care if you have walked on water. The light you have brought to others can quickly turn into perceived darkness when you need a miracle for yourself.

I have heard it said God turned his back on Jesus at the cross—that he was unable to maintain eye contact with his Son due to the overwhelming amount of sin Jesus willfully took upon himself. I, however, am not convinced. Perhaps we have mistaken God's timing for God's absence. If sin blocked God's view of his children, the earth would currently appear uninhabited (Romans 3:23). For the record, if we have to be sinless for God to see us, call me invisible.

God can see you no matter the circumstances. Darkness may have covered the land for the last three hours Jesus hung on the cross but darkness did not cover God's eyes. God wears night vision goggles. In fact, he never takes them off. If sin and trouble ever blinded God from seeing you, he would find a way to read your life in Braille. Even the Old Testament prophets held this truth:

> "Be strong and courageous. Do not be afraid or terrified because of them, for the LORD your God goes with you; he will never leave you nor forsake you." (Deuteronomy 31:6)

In my opinion, God did not turn away from Jesus, and God has not turned away from you. He has not forsaken you. God loves you. As the proud father of two sons, I can tell you there is no power in heaven or hell that would cause me to turn my back on either of them in their time of need. Since I am created in the image and likeness of God, the only logical conclusion is he would do the same for his children. God's viewpoint never changes. He stands, eyes wide open, on the balconies of heaven keeping watch over the entire earth (Proverbs 15:3). Our viewpoint, however, constantly changes. King David said it best:

> I'm an open book to you; even from a distance you know what I'm thinking. You know when I leave and when I get back. You know everything I'm going to say before I start the first sentence. I look behind me and you're there, then up ahead and you're there, too—your reassuring presence, coming and going. This is too much, too wonderful—I can't take it all in! Is there any place I can go to avoid your Spirit? to be out of your sight? If I climb to the sky, you're there! If I go underground, you're there! If I flew on morning's wings to the far western horizon, you'd find me in a minute—you're already there waiting! (Psalm 139:2–10 MSG)

There is no shortage of exclamation points in David's description of God's presence. Nothing, not even the darkness David invited on the night Bathsheba came to visit, could cause God to take his eye off him. As David stated, it really is too wonderful to take in. During blackout, we are tempted to believe God's notable absence is why we can't get out of our mess. Perhaps there's more to the story. At least consider the possibility. Maybe you have been overlooking the obvious.

Reflection Journal: Today, evaluate the true condition of your life. How has God been with you the entire time?

_____

_____

_____

_____

_____

Fear Blocker

"So we say with confidence, 'The Lord is my helper; I will not be afraid. What can mere mortals do to me?' Remember your leaders, who spoke the word of God to you. Consider the outcome of their way of life and imitate their faith. Jesus Christ is the same yesterday, today, and forever" (Hebrews 13:6–8).

▨ ▨ ▨

Delay Doesn't Mean Denial

DON'T MISTAKE FEELING abandoned by God for your disapproval of how he is handling your life. Today, embrace the "wait."

Key Verse: "But they that wait upon the LORD shall renew their strength; they shall mount up with wings as eagles; they shall run, and not be weary; and they shall walk, and not faint" (Isaiah 40:31 KJV).

Children are not very good at waiting patiently and worse, when not getting what they want. But good parents realize timing is crucial. My boys haven't always understood what their mother and I were doing, even when it was in their best interest. For example, I don't care if they occasionally have a hot fudge sundae. In fact, I am often the one doing the scooping. After all, if they're eating ice cream, so am I! I do, however, care about the timing and the amount. Ice cream before dinner doesn't work at my house. I am not trying to diminish or downplay what's got you shaken by talking about something as unimportant as dessert. I am only establishing that in regard to the relationship between parents and children, delay doesn't always mean denial, and a different approach is sometimes best, even when it's not fully understood.

As a child of God, you must learn to trust him with the timing issues of life and not throw a fit when something doesn't work out exactly the way you wanted (or in the timeframe you're demanding). I have been guilty of that kind of behavior. Now, I refuse to be that child who falls kicking and screaming to the floor when they don't get their way.

Occasionally, your heavenly Father will say, "Wait." And not because he doesn't love you, but because he wants the best for you. Perhaps, God isn't meeting your expectations because his plan is to surpass them. I am quite sure it took every ounce of divine restraint to keep God from showing up early when Jesus felt forsaken. A premature rescue, however, would not have turned a carpenter from Nazareth into the captain of our salvation (Hebrews 2:10). An early departure out of the dark would have reduced the Lion of Judah (Revelation 5:5) into the liar the Pharisees accused him of being. Wrapped in darkness and overwhelmed by the sick feeling of being forsaken, Jesus had to wait it out. King Solomon offers wise counsel on the topic: "Hope deferred makes the heart sick, but a longing fulfilled is a tree of life" (Proverbs 13:12).

In hope, you believe better days are on the horizon. In your mind you see God, muscles rippling, standing on the edge of your darkness with a lasso around the sun. If the darkness won't budge, he will certainly pull the light into it. What you have been praying for is just a short tug away for such a powerful God. He could do it. Without a can of spinach, he could do it! In the blink of an eye, he is capable of giving you what you so desperately long for.

However, when the days turn into weeks and the weeks into months without a definitive answer or response, heart sickness can set in. The enemy is well aware of this and is working to get you into a spiritual hospital bed. It's easy to feel heart broken when what you want most is seemingly being kept from you. Heart sickness thrives in the dark and can create the worst kind of anxiety. When God isn't doing what you're begging him to do, it's frustrating, but like Isaiah promised, it's also the path to renewed strength.

What you see as denial, is more than likely God acting as a good father. He loves you too much to allow your future to become second-rate. It's the wait that eventually reveals the promise and gives you those eagle wings. Don't miss your flight!

Reflection Journal: What will you do to keep your strength up during the wait?

Fear Blocker

"But blessed is the one who trusts in the LORD, whose confidence is in him. They will be like a tree planted by the water that sends out its roots by the stream. It does not fear when heat comes; its leaves are always green. It has no worries in a year of drought and never fails to bear fruit" (Jeremiah 17:7–8).

■ ■ ■

God's Terms and God's Conditions

ASK YOURSELF: IS my hope in what I hope will happen or is my hope in God no matter what happens? It's easy to confuse the two. I am not suggesting God will never give you what you want. I am merely pointing out God knows what is best and must be trusted with the outcome.

Key Verse: "Listen, GOD, I'm calling at the top of my lungs: 'Be good to me! Answer me!' When my heart whispered, 'Seek God,' my whole being replied, 'I'm seeking him!' Don't hide from me now! You've always been right there for me; don't turn your back on me now. Don't throw me out, don't abandon me; you've always kept the door open. My father and mother walked out and left me, but GOD took me in" (Psalm 27:7–10 MSG).

God very much wants to bring you out of every place of pain and fearfulness. He gets no pleasure in watching his children struggle with the complicated issues of life. Like a hungry tiger ready to pounce on its prey, God anticipates the opportunity to jump into the abyss and ferociously attack what's attacking you. He, however, will not sign a terms and conditions contract. Have you seen those? Occasionally, while shopping online or filling out some type of application on my computer,

I am not allowed to move forward until I have agreed to all the terms and conditions. It's simple, really—all I have to do is read twenty-five pages of font so small you need a magnifying glass to see it. I will confess—I never read the terms and conditions. I just check the box agreeing to them. I bet you do that too. I do this even though it is not wise. For all I know, I could be signing over my firstborn or giving them permission to empty my bank account. After all, it's their terms and conditions I am consenting to. I need to start paying attention to the fine print, instead of just carelessly checking the box.

God will not check the box agreeing to your terms and conditions. He doesn't need your advice on how to handle times of agitation. He only needs your obedience, worship, and cooperation while he is arranging your resurrection!

When the lights are off and your worst fears lurk in every direction, it's of the highest importance you seek God's help, rather than tell God how to help. God has not forgotten about you. He isn't going to turn his back while you slowly slip into a chasm of despair. Your responsibility is to seek him. David tells us why:

> The LORD is a refuge for the oppressed, a stronghold in times of trouble. Those who know your name trust in you, for you, LORD, have never forsaken those who seek you. (Psalm 9:9–10)

God is a safe house for the battered and a shelter during bad times. You must trust him with the future even when things appear to be at a standstill or worse, going in the wrong direction. God is incapable of forsaking those who seek him. It isn't in his nature to turn away from a reaching heart. You can feel forsaken when seeking God's hands becomes more important to you than seeking his face.

Today, as you write in your journal, make a list of terms and conditions you have placed on God. Be honest about what you have been demanding he do in order for you to move forward and be happy. Afterward, tear them up.

Reflection Journal: Terms and conditions.

Fear Blocker

"Therefore I tell you, do not worry about your life, what you will eat or drink; or about your body, what you will wear. Is not life more than food, and the body more than clothes? Look at the birds of the air; they do not sow or reap or store away in barns, and yet the heavenly Father feeds them. Are you not more valuable than they? Can any one of you by worrying add a single hour to your life?" (Matthew 6:25–27).

■ ■ ■

Part V

Beacons of Light

- "It started when God said, 'Light up the darkness!' and our lives filled up with light as we saw and understood God in the face of Christ, all bright and beautiful" (2 Corinthians 4:6 MSG).

- "Every good and perfect gift is from above, coming down from the Father of the heavenly lights, who does not change like shifting shadows" (James 1:17).

- "You, LORD, keep my lamp burning; my God turns my darkness into light" (Psalm 18:28).

A Story of Unshakable Faith

After three years of marriage, Eric and Tiffany filed for divorce. Counseling proved ineffective and the situation was quickly spiraling out of control. Eric was an angry and abusive man who drank too much and had no relationship with their infant son, Braxton. Fearing for her safety, Tiffany's only choice was to get herself and her baby as far away from Eric as possible. After the divorce was final, she agreed to give Eric supervised visitation twice a month. A mistake she would later regret.

Over the next four years, as agreed, Eric did show up to see Braxton but never made any real effort to connect with him. To complicate things further, Eric continued to live a reckless lifestyle. Despite Tiffany's best efforts to reassure Braxton, he was still afraid of his dad and often cried on the day of the visitation.

"It was miserable. I hated seeing my sweet little boy thrown into such turmoil. Before we arrived at the park to meet Eric, Braxton would hide in the floorboard. He was terrified and there was nothing that I could do about it," Tiffany explained. Eventually, the visits became shorter and less frequent. Tiffany was beginning to think Eric might finally sign away his parental rights and stop creating havoc for their son. Eric had other plans. When Braxton turned five, even though Eric never spent any time alone with him, he filed for joint physical custody. After months of battling in court, to everyone's disbelief his request was granted.

Tiffany said, "I felt devastated, numb, and in complete shock. My worst fear had come true. I knew what kind of man he was and the thought of Braxton being forced into Eric's lifestyle was unbelievable. This was my 'why' moment. Why would God allow this? Surely there was another way."

Over the next few months Braxton went to Eric's home. It was just as Tiffany feared. He began to have problems at school, accidents in his pants, and night terrors. Things weren't getting better and God wasn't listening. The more she prayed for God to intervene the worse the situation became. She knew God had a plan but what was it and why was it taking so long?

Tiffany explains her journey through blackout: "I began seeking God rather than seeking what I wanted God to do. During those times when Braxton was with his dad, I put on worship music and turned it into a time of sowing in praise, rather than a time of sorrow. As a result, I soon realized that God wanted me to forgive Eric and release all the bitterness that I had toward him in my heart. So, I began praying for him. I broke down and cried out for his soul. I had to change my image of Eric. I started to see him not as the terrible man he was, but as the suicidal little boy he once described to me. It was difficult at first and, in the beginning, all I could say was, 'God, I pray for him,' but eventually I meant it."

In less than six months Eric signed away his parental rights. Tiffany left me with this thought: "I wasn't waiting on God. He was waiting on me. Once I was willing to accept what God was doing in my life and, in obedience, forgive Eric, the answer quickly came."

Tiffany's story is proof that when you feel forsaken, you're not forsaken. God is arranging the future according to his terms and conditions, not yours. The timing and the method belong to him alone. God not only answered Tiffany's prayer regarding her son, he also used his terms and conditions to help her release the poison she had in her spirit toward Eric.

PART VI
WHEN THE CUP WON'T PASS

*Then Jesus went with them to a garden
called Gethsemane and told his disciples,
"Stay here while I go over there and pray."
Taking Peter and the two sons of Zebedee,
he plunged into an agonizing sorrow. Then
he said, "This sorrow is crushing my life out.
Stay here and keep vigil with me." Going a little
ahead, he fell on his face, praying, "My Father,
if there is any other way, get me out of this.
But please, not what I want. You, what do you
want?" (Matthew 26:36–39 MSG)*

"We need never be ashamed of our tears."
—Charles Dickens, Great Expectations

Uncoiled

YOU MAY STILL be under the full crushing weight of your dilemma and praying for relief. Refuse to be distracted by thoughts of defeat. You may feel struck down but you cannot be destroyed. The enemy will try and put the squeeze on you but you're uncrushable.

Key Verse: "We are hard pressed on every side, but not crushed; perplexed but not in despair; persecuted, but not abandoned; struck down, but not destroyed" (2 Corinthians 4:8–9).

As I sit writing today's material, I find myself unusually distracted. Typically, I am laser focused and have a well-thought-out plan for obtaining my word count. However, a story from Brazil keeps reoccurring in my newsfeed. I'm trying hard to ignore it and find my spiritual groove, but my eyes keep glancing over to the screen on my right. It appears a group of miners found something unbelievable. If curiosity killed the cat, I would be a dead cat! I have to know what it is.

Be right back. Wow! Apparently, a thirty-three-foot-long anaconda was just discovered at a construction site in South America. There are pictures of the beast and reputable news sources have confirmed this snake is, in fact, real. It measures three feet across the back and is the largest snake ever captured alive. After looking at the pictures and seeing the monster hanging from a construction crane, I have concluded nightmares have nightmares about this snake! Now I know why God arranged my schedule so I would write this particular information on the day of this breaking story. There is a huge (thirty-three-foot-long) lesson here!

Like the monster snake, life has coils. I bet you already knew that. Blackout wraps you and waits for you to silently suffocate. It squeezes, anxiously anticipating one final breath so it can feed on your lost hope. Fortunately for you and me, our God is an expert snake handler. He's been wrangling snakes since the beginning of time. When life coils around you, he springs into action. While he may not deliver you from every season of sorrow, he will certainly stick with you.

The lights were flickering on Jesus when he fell on his face and said, "This sorrow is crushing my life out" (Matthew 26:38 MSG). Darkness coiled tighter and tighter around the Savior as he poured out his worry and anxiety before God. Like Jesus, you can be terrified and trusting at the same time. Your feelings about your dilemma have no bearing on God's willingness to help you. When life was putting the squeeze on Jesus, he said, "Get me out of here." Like a vise grip, he felt things tightening.

It's one thing when your friends won't join you in the garden for tea and a few easy-bake prayers. It's another thing to feel all alone in the darkest circumstances without any real support team to pray with or encourage you. Jesus didn't invite the disciples to the garden to look at the flowers or chase butterflies. He invited them there to pray for strength—his strength. It's abundantly clear they did not grasp the severity of the situation. Jesus agonized, while they dozed.

Scripture says Jesus was deeply distressed. He wasn't just having a bad day. For example: He wasn't mad because the waitress got his order wrong. He wasn't stressed out over a three-hour traffic jam. No, he was overwhelmed by the torture of what he knew was coming and the death facing him. Have you ever wondered what deeply distressed looked like on Jesus? I have. One thing is for sure—he didn't get mad, scream, and throw things. He didn't collapse under the load and decide God didn't care about him. Deeply distressed on Jesus probably looked a little different than it sometimes does on you and me. I will be the first to admit when facing deep sorrow, I'm not at my best, nor do I always feel like God is by my side. My feelings, however, do not change reality, and reality is God will get in the coils of dilemma with his children.

Unfortunately, life happens to us all. It rains on the just and the unjust (Matthew 5:45). Preacher and prostitute face difficulty. The life of Jesus proves that occasionally we will have to go through some pain and turbulent times. Jesus didn't want to drink the cup and neither do we. The cup Jesus drank was filled with every sin ever committed or will ever be committed. It is unimaginable to comprehend what he was willing to ingest so you and I could find our way to his father. Every rape, murder, lie, act of adultery, gossip, rebellion, and theft—just to name a few—were contained in the cup.

Your cup may be filled with divorce, bankruptcy, disease, depression, disappointment, and loss. The point is, even children of God have to drink something from time to time that tastes bitter. The truth is, no matter how much you want it to, sometimes the cup won't pass. Like Jesus, there will be instances when you must face what you would rather hand off to someone else.

Reflection Journal: Your circumstances cannot change the future God has in store. What does "deeply distressed" usually look like on you. How will you change this?

_____

_____

_____

_____

_____

Fear Blocker

"Anxiety in a man's heart weights him down, but a good word makes him glad" (Proverbs 12:25 ESV).

▪ ▪ ▪

The Oil of Gladness

YOU CAN USE the shambles of yesterday to pave the road leading you into a better tomorrow. God doesn't create pain in the lives of his followers but he will use stressful situations to help them gain a new advantage. Keep walking. Keep believing.

Key Verse: "To comfort all who mourn, and provide for those who grieve in Zion—to bestow on them a crown of beauty for ashes, the oil of joy instead of mourning, and a garment of praise instead of a spirit of despair" (Isaiah 61:2b–3a).

The garden of Gethsemane, where Jesus prayed the night before he was betrayed, was more than a nice place to take a stroll to eye the local scenery. Gethsemane literally means, oil press. This is more than likely a reference to the amount of oil gathered from the olive trees growing there. Here, the darkness was trying to steamroll Jesus by forcing him into isolation.

In the same way, circumstances beyond your control will try and press the oil of God's presence out of you. If what's got you rattled can refocus your attention and get your mind on everything going wrong, it will be difficult for you to believe for better days, let alone, incredible days.

Maybe you feel like a bug under the foot of your problem. Life is coming down hard on you and you believe you have reached the limit of what you can handle. You feel all alone—like everyone is getting on with their lives, while you're swirling in chaos. Jesus knows exactly how you feel because he has been there too.

Keep in mind, God doesn't cause pain. Sin does that. Stress, worry, and anxiety are a result of the fact we live in a fallen world. God, however, will use every difficult situation to strengthen your faith. When it's dark and the cup won't pass, like Jesus, you're in the press. I know it hurts and you would never choose to be in this position, but God has a plan. The press isn't designed to flatten you or give you a nervous breakdown. It's being used by God to expand the borders of your happiness and future blessings, as you learn to trust him while experiencing pain and heartbreak. You're not being crushed to death. You're being pressed to life!

Gethsemane was God's way of preparing Jesus for what was to come. Here, Jesus prayed in agony until his sweat became as "great drops of blood" (Luke 22:44 ESV). When life puts the squeeze on you, something will be pressed out. It can be doubt, despair, and a declaration of how unfair God is or it can be an absolute refusal to allow the despair to get the better of you. Blackout intends to press you until there's nothing left but mourning. What if instead of mourning over your situation, you did something unexpected by turning the tables and allowing the oil of joy to flow (Isaiah 61:3)? You may be thinking, *That sounds great, Larry, and in a perfect world maybe I could exchange all this madness for some gladness but right now, I don't think I can.* The apostle Paul offers great insight:

> "May the God of hope fill you with all joy and peace as you trust in him, so that you may over-

flow with hope by the power of the Holy Spirit." (Romans 15:13)

Even in the midst of blackout, the oil vats can overflow! Not with tension and heartache but with joy and peace as you trust in God. Those times of no flow in your life are actually opportunities for future overflow! According to Paul, trust is the key component to finding hope and joy. God is not asking you to slay a giant, attend every prayer meeting within fifty miles or to even appear to have it all together. He is only asking you to trust him. If life is bearing down on your faith and trying to flatten your confidence, this is a perfect opportunity for you to be filled with joy and peace as you place your hope in God's ability to provide the overflow you've been lacking.

I think it's worth noting, olive oil was often used in biblical times as a light source. All alone in the dark, Jesus was surrounded by what was used as fuel for lamps. In a moment of overwhelming blackout, a light source was at his fingertips the entire time, and light is at your fingertips as well.

Jesus knew what was coming. It was inevitable. It wasn't the wood or the nails that had him rattled. It was the crushing weight of sin he dreaded. The lights were going out and all he could do was prepare the best he knew how. The reflection journal will be especially important today. You, no doubt, have a few things in your life that make you smile—things causing your oil vats to overflow. Focus on those things.

Reflection Journal: Make a list of the things in your life that make you glad. How will you use those things to remind you of how joyful life can be?

Fear Blocker

"What, then, shall we say in response to these things? If God is for us, who can be against us? He who did not spare his own Son, but gave him up for us all—how will he not also, along with him, graciously give us all things? Who will bring any charge against those whom God has chosen? It is God who justifies. Who is the one who condemns? No one. Christ Jesus, who died—more than that, who was raised to life—is at the right hand of God and is also interceding for us" (Romans 8:31–34).

■ ■ ■

When Your Back Is to the Wall, Remember His Back Was to the Cross

THE WALL YOU'RE up against is no match for the one who faced the cross—destroying death. You can keep your chin up, knowing God will not disappoint you.

Key Verse: "He went away a second time and prayed, 'My Father, if it is not possible for this cup to be taken away unless I drink it, may your will be done'" (Matthew 26:42).

Jesus readied himself—and so can you. He knew in the end, he wouldn't be disappointed with the outcome. Jesus didn't want to drink from the cup but he needed to. Without the cup, there would have been no forgiveness of sins, healing for our sicknesses and diseases or the arrival of the Holy Spirit. I am also convinced Jesus was thinking about the message contained in the book of Romans when he consented to the coming crucifixion:

> Not only so, but we also glory in our suffer-
> ings, because we know that suffering produces

perseverance; perseverance, character; and character, hope. And hope does not put us to shame. (Romans 5:3–5)

The journey into any place worth going usually begins with suffering. I can tell you from personal experience, what has cut me the deepest, has also been my most effective tool in ministry. The pain I've endured has shaped my life in a far greater way than my successes. Jesus clearly understood suffering is the path to perseverance, character, and hope. Simply put, suffering is a launching pad. God is not trying to drown you in darkness when the cup won't pass. Rather, he is working to launch you into your intended destiny. I know it might not seem like that is what is happening in your life, but don't forget—before an arrow can be launched, it has to be pulled back.

Remember what Jesus said: "Not as I will, but as you will" (Matthew 26:39).

In your mind (and mine), it's easy to believe if you always got what you wanted and everything turned out exactly the way you pictured, that would be utopia. The cup Jesus didn't want to drink tells us a different story. The cross wasn't what Jesus wanted. In fact, it was the last thing he wanted and for good reason. I am sure his flesh was giving him some alternatives that sounded a lot better than what he was about to go through. Jesus could have resisted the cup and decided drinking it was too hard. Instead, he decided if the Father brought him to it, he would certainly bring him through it.

There are many difficult things in life you will not be able to escape. They are your "cup that won't pass." When this happens, it is imperative you follow the example established by Jesus. Falling on his face, in agonizing sorrow, feeling like life was being crushed out of him, he said, "Not as I will, but as you will." God never wills for his children to suffer. He only wills that when life puts the squeeze on them, he be allowed to partner with them in their suffering.

Blackout may have coiled around you, but God has also wrapped himself around you. Allow the tightening you feel to be God's strong arms wrapping you in comfort. God wants to turn the squeeze into a hug—a hug from him. Since you already have a cup, let's make a toast. Here's to your future!

Reflection Journal: As difficult as it might be, make a list of all the ways you can rejoice in your suffering. Don't think about the pain, concentrate on the promotion.

_____

_____

_____

_____

_____

Fear Blocker

"But the Advocate, the Holy Spirit, whom the Father will send in my name, will teach you all things and remind you of everything I have said to you. Peace I leave with you; my peace I give to you. I do not give to you as the world gives. Do not let your hearts be troubled and do not be afraid" (John 14:26–27).

■ ■ ■

Part VI

Beacons of Light

- "But you are a chosen people, a royal priesthood, a holy nation, God's special possession, that you may declare the praises of him who called you out of darkness into his wonderful light" (1 Peter 2:9).

- "But friends, you're not in the dark, so how could you be taken off guard by any of this? You're sons of the Light, daughters of the Day. We live under wide open skies and know where we stand. So let's not sleepwalk through life like those others. Let's keep our eyes open and be smart. People sleep at night and get drunk at night. But not us! Walk out into the daylight sober, dressed up in faith, love, and the hope of salvation" (1 Thessalonians 5:4–11 MSG).

- "We couldn't be more sure of what we saw and heard—God's glory, God's voice. The prophetic Word was confirmed to us. You'll do well to keep focusing on it. It's the one light you have in a dark time as you wait for daybreak and the rising of the Morning Star in your hearts" (2 Peter 1:19 MSG).

A Story of Unshakable Faith

Tony—an entrepreneur, husband, and father—finally realized his dream of owning his own real-estate company. The housing market was booming and his small business quickly began to grow. Things were definitely looking up as the opportunity to buy affordable properties of his own began pouring in. Tony never expected the bottom to fall out, but that's what happened when the housing market crashed. In one month, he not only lost all his contracts but also the ability to make the payment on his loans.

"Every morning I woke up just trying to keep my head above the water. My days were filled with calls from lenders. There was no way I could pay them all back. I was in a hole of despair and it seemed like the more I tried, the worse things became," he said.

In spite of how bad things got, Tony and his wife continued to trust God with their finances. He said, "There were weeks when we knew that if we wrote the tithe check to our church, there wouldn't be enough left over to make our house payment. We tithed anyway. We believed that by honoring God with what we had left, he would help us get out of the financial mess we were in. We knew that God would not disappoint us."

As a result, the next few months were filled with unexpected opportunities and financial blessings. In a relatively short amount of time, most of the debt was wiped out. Tony never filed bankruptcy. He left me with these words: "Even though I made a few mistakes along the way, God always honors obedience. As we were obedient with what we had left, God made up the rest. He didn't disappoint us."

PART VII
WHEN LIFE DOESN'T MAKE SENSE

When they came back from the tomb, they told all these things to the Eleven and to all the others. It was Mary Magdalene, Joanna, Mary the mother of James, and the others with them who told this to the apostles. But they did not believe the women because their words seemed to them like nonsense. (Luke 24:9–11)

"What gives me the most hope every day is God's grace; knowing that his grace is going to give me the strength for whatever I face, knowing that nothing is a surprise to God."
—Rick Warren

DAY
19

It Doesn't Have
to Make Sense to Be True

JESUS KNOWS HOW a lack of understanding can be frustrating and at times, overwhelming. Today, trust him with the puzzle pieces still not fitting. Believe he knows how to put everything back together and is working to shift the odds in your favor.

Key Verse: "Jesus answered, 'You don't understand now what I'm doing, but it will be clear enough to you later'" (John 13:7 MSG).

Short and stubby, the bumblebee doesn't look very flight worthy. In fact, in the 1930s, French entomologist August Magnan noted the insect's flight was actually impossible. He stated the law of physics simply doesn't allow a creature of such disproportion to lift itself off the ground. Yet, the bumblebee can certainly fly. Its ability to defy basic aerodynamics doesn't make sense, however, our little black-and-yellow friend can soar through the air with ease. Trust me, I know. Once while clearing a pasture of rocks, I disturbed a bumblebee nest. I was stung over ten times before jumping in the pond! I wish August Magnan was there that day. We could have discussed the impossibility of the bumblebee's flight while running for our lives.

When the women returned from the empty tomb with news of a resurrected Savior, it didn't add up. Yet, it was obviously true. And it should have made perfect sense; after all, Jesus told them time and time again that while death did have the power to take him, it did not have power to keep him. Perhaps, they remembered the violent way in which he died and thought, no one, not even the Master can recover from such an end. Whatever the case, it's apparent the disciples weren't being very cooperative while going through what they didn't understand.

Even Peter, one of Jesus's best friends and closest ministry partners, was puzzled by how life was unfolding. Luke was quick to point this out:

> But Peter jumped to his feet and ran to the tomb.
> He stooped to look in and saw a few grave clothes,
> that's all. He walked away puzzled, shaking his
> head. (Luke 24:12 MSG)

As you move through life, you will no doubt experience seasons that leave you shaking your head. Unlike the disciples, who were warned about the approaching blackout, you, more than likely, will never see it coming. It will be a surprise attack.

This wasn't the first time the disciples had an opportunity to question the direction and teaching of Jesus. Let's face it, whenever Jesus was thrown into the mix, not much made sense—yet it always turned out better than expected. From his virgin birth to his empty tomb, the questions marks are piled high. During blackout, two and two rarely add up to four.

How can you trust God with the future when the present is in such disrepair? There have been times when I've told God

I felt like a fool for ever trusting him in the first place. While that's hard for me to admit, it's the truth. I truly believe you and I are at our most vulnerable when we lack understanding. God wants to help you make sense out of the things not making sense.

From the very beginning, the disciples thought Jesus would surely deliver them from Roman tyranny and set up an earthly kingdom—he would silence the Pharisees and prove once and for all he was God. That's not what happened. Perhaps you feel like the disciples. You were headed in a good direction and felt positively about the future but suddenly the bottom fell out and now you're struggling just to keep it together. You love God but you don't understand him right now. You feel like you're a victim of circumstance and a martyr dying for a cause you don't even believe in. You constantly ask yourself, "Why is this happening?"

When life takes a turn, what if the detour is the route forward? I'm guessing you're skeptical and have more interest in going backward than forward. After all, when you look down the road ahead of you, all you can see right now are potholes filled with pain and more valleys than hilltops. At least the highway facing yesterday was smooth at times. If you feel that way, I pose an important question: Have you considered allowing God to use your detour? I can assure you even when you don't understand and life isn't making sense, God has a well-thought-out plan. Nothing shocks God. He never looks down in wide-eyed amazement at the degree of your difficulties. He is never caught off guard by what catches you off guard. I'm not sure how often my name is mentioned in heaven. I am, however, positive God never says, "Did you see what happened to Larry? He's never coming back from that!" On the contrary,

I can hear God saying, "The lights went out on Larry today, finally an opportunity for me to shine!"

Reflection Journal: What's not making sense in your life? Be specific.

_____

_____

_____

_____

_____

Fear Blocker

"Strengthen the feeble hands, steady the knees that give way; say to those with fearful hearts, 'Be strong, do not fear; your God will come, he will come with vengeance, with divine retribution he will come to save you'" (Isaiah 35:3–5).

■ ■ ■

God Saw It Coming

GOD CAN SEE what has been keeping you up at night. He knows why your stomach is in knots. He knew about your trouble, long before you found out about it.

Key Verse: "David said it all: 'I saw God before me for all time. Nothing can shake me; he's right by my side. I'm glad from the inside out, ecstatic; I've pitched my tent in the land of hope. I'll never even smell the stench of death. You've got my feet on the life-path, with your face shining sun-joy all around'" (Acts 2:25–28 MSG).

God's purposes for your life are set. They aren't affected by the depths of what has been dragging you under. In less than two months, the same disciple who shook his head in confusion at the tomb of Jesus, offers what could easily be the best advice ever given when you're overtaken by despair. Listen as the apostle Peter tells the crowd gathered after the day of Pentecost, what was actually happening behind the scenes when the sun stopped shining:

> "Fellow Israelites, listen to this: Jesus of Nazareth was a man accredited by God to you by miracles, wonders and signs, which God did among

you through him, as you yourselves know. This
man was handed over to you by God's deliberate
plan and foreknowledge; and you, with the help
of wicked men, put him to death by nailing him
to the cross. But God raised him from the dead,
freeing him from the agony of death, because it
was impossible for death to keep its hold on him."
(Acts 2:22–24)

When trapped in what you can't fix, remember darkness
is no match for God. He, alone, can untie death's ropes. When
you're pinned down, reach up. God's set purpose is working to
free you from the agony of a broken heart. Even when you're
facing the loss of something that can never be replaced, you can
confidently move forward knowing God will not leave you on
the back roads of pain and suffering. The detour may have left
you feeling miles from nowhere, but the road in front of you
will lead you out.

The apostle Peter was quick to point out, God's set purpose
and foreknowledge concerning what was going to happen to
Jesus went hand in hand. The nails, whip, and the unbelievably
heavy weight of sin were all a part of the plan of salvation. I
realize this is a subject often skipped over. It's uncomfortable
and causes us to question. If God can see the darkness heading
in our direction, why doesn't he step in front of it? Maybe you
feel like a dear woman I recently met. Her grandson was just
killed in a wreck, less than two miles from her home. She said,
"Larry, why did this happen and why did God allow it?" I will
admit I stumbled a little in my response.

As I have already stated in earlier chapters, I explained to
her God does not cause catastrophe in the lives of his children.

The fact her grandson was killed was not God's fault and if given the choice, God would have spared her the pain. The garden of Eden is a perfect example of the kind of life God envisions for us—a life free of death and darkness. Sin put thorns on roses, and we have felt the poke and poison ever since. This earth is no longer our home. After Adam and Eve sinned, our capacity to find comfort here was greatly diminished. Heaven is our home, and the problems we encounter in our everyday lives should make us homesick.

The foreknowledge of God is not a slap in the face. It only proves that once God knows the sun is about to stop shining, he immediately begins working on the dawn of a new day. It was true for Jesus and it is true for you as well. Your rescue may involve the love and support offered by others or the warm blanket of comfort thrown over you by the Holy Spirit. This book is even part of your healing. God saw the cross long before Jesus was nailed to it.

Will you be like Jesus, who couldn't be shaken, or will you end up like so many others with crumbled foundations? While walking through the graveyard of death, it is possible for your feet to be firmly planted on a life-path. Just like with Jesus, the enemy is working hard to get you to forget God is the only good thing, in every bad thing.

Reflection Journal: Even though you're still working your way to the light, what have you seen God doing (along the way) to prove he always had a plan?

Fear Blocker

"Then Jesus declared, 'I am the bread of life. He who comes to me will never go hungry, and he who believes in me will never be thirsty.'" (John 6:35–36).

■ ■ ■

God Can Handle It

GOD CAN CERTAINLY handle whatever life throws in your direction. He is still the God who raises the dead. He cannot be bullied by death.

Key Verse: "We felt like we'd been sent to death row, that it was all over for us. As it turned out, it was the best thing that could have happened. Instead of trusting in our own strength or wits to get out of it, we were forced to trust God totally—not a bad idea since he's the God who raises the dead!" (2 Corinthians 1:9 MSG).

The apostle Paul had a lot to say about the confusing conditions of life. Sunless days piled high with despair were something he was very familiar with and, like in the above verse, often wrote about. Paul was thrown in prison, bitten by a snake, shipwrecked, abandoned by team members, and even stoned to near death—all while pursuing God's will. Paul was the poster child for what to do when the once clearly defined lines of life get blurry.

How did he keep moving forward in the face of such chaos? The answer is easy to spot as you read his writings. Paul used the resurrection of Jesus as an example when disclosing his private thoughts during days of distress. He often looked back at what didn't make sense at the time, and by examining God's faithfulness, he was able to stand strong. I think the best example of this is found in Paul's second letter to the Corinthian church. Here, Paul explains to the Corinthians how God's faithfulness can be seen in three time zones: past, present, and future.

If you disregard God's faithfulness in the past—the future probably looks bleak. Paul learned a lot about the purposes of God while in Asia:

> We don't want you in the dark, friends, about how hard it was when all this came down on us in Asia province. It was so bad we didn't think we were going to make it. (2 Corinthians 1:8 MSG)

Considering the relentless pounding Paul went through, you know it is serious business when he says something is so bad he thought he might not make it out. When your world is twirling and your future seems a mess—so twisted it can never be untangled—you too can believe life is over. Paul, honestly, felt like the plan of God was somehow altered and the future was so compromised it could never be salvaged, let alone blessed. Thankfully, the story doesn't end there. Like most good books, life comes with a few cliff-hangers, and in those moments of suspense, you can become scared. Fear is trying to get you to forget God still makes the crooked places of life straight (Isaiah 45:2).

It can be difficult to trust God while you're waiting to see how something is going to turn out. When Paul thought he wasn't going to make it, he was forced to put his trust completely in God. Something, he admits, he should have been doing all along. He implies that in the past, he occasionally relied upon his own strength and wits but not this time. This time he was dependent upon the God who raises the dead. The results were incredible:

He has delivered us from such a deadly peril, and
he will deliver us. On him we have set our hope that
he will continue to deliver us. (2 Corinthians 1:10)

Once removed from the dark corners of Asia, Paul boldly proclaims, "God has delivered us, God is currently delivering us, and God will continue to deliver us." God is not bound by time. His faithfulness can be seen in the past and present, which indicates he can also be trusted with the future. If God could raise Jesus back to life, he could easily handle anything Paul found distressing. Likewise, God can also handle whatever currently has you in a panic. Just because something doesn't make sense at the time, doesn't mean it won't make sense *in* time. God is a time traveler. He can reach back into the confusion of yesterday and use every tragic thing that tried to take you out, as opportunity to lift you up. He can show up in the shadows of your current crisis proving yet again the Son has your back. The future is no match for the Alpha and Omega, the Beginning and the End, and the First and the Last (Revelation 22:13).

Reflection Journal: How has God been faithful to you in the past? What has he already brought you out of?

Fear Blocker

"I will praise the LORD, who counsels me; even at night my heart instructs me. I keep my eyes always on the LORD. With him at my right hand, I will not be shaken. Therefore my heart is glad and my tongue rejoices; my body also will rest secure, because you will not abandon me to the realm of the dead, nor will you let your faithful one see decay. You make known to me the path of life; you will fill me with joy in your presence, with eternal pleasures at your right hand" (Psalm 16:7–11).

❋ ❋ ❋

Part VII

Beacons of Light

- "When Jesus spoke again to the people, he said, 'I am the light of the world. Whoever follows me will never walk in darkness, but will have the light of life'" (John 8:12).

- "Men and women who have lived wisely and well will shine brilliantly, like the cloudless, star-strewn night skies. And those who put others on the right path to life will glow like the stars forever" (Daniel 12:3 MSG).

- "You're a fountain of cascading light, and you open our eyes to light" (Psalm 36:9 MSG).

A Story of Unshakable Faith

Susan grew up in a loving upper middle-class home, a picture of suburbia. After college, she became a school teacher and eventually, the director of a preschool. She married and had two children. At the age of forty-one, she accepted Christ as her savior. After a long, rewarding career in education, Susan retired. She said, "Even though I loved my job and could have easily stayed, I felt like God had something else in mind for me. I didn't know what, I only sensed there was something more. I prayed for guidance and committed myself to whatever God required. At the time, I had no idea what I was getting myself into."

With no prior symptoms, at the age of fifty-seven, Susan was diagnosed with late onset bipolar one disorder. She was hallucinating, delusional, and manic. Because of her deranged state, her family was forced to put her under psychiatric care, but unfortunately it wasn't effective. Her symptoms only amplified. She was paranoid, snapping in and out of reality, and even had her family convinced her husband was cheating on her. Susan was seeing, smelling, and hearing things that weren't real and, on more than one occasion, she was even trying to cast demons out of herself. Her family had no choice but to hospitalize her.

After months of medical care, complete dependency upon God, and an absolute refusal to give up, Susan slowly began finding her way back to her old self. At the request of her doctor, she went to a National Alliance on Mental Illness support group (N.A.M.I.). "At first, I didn't feel like I belonged. After all, these people weren't like me. Or so I thought. I didn't want to go back, but I couldn't stay away," she said.

Soon it became clear to Susan God wanted her to start a N.A.M.I. support group in her hometown—something she would have never considered before her illness. Now, years later, Susan is completely healed of her mental lapse and is leading a thriving mental health care group. Susan left me with this thought, "What looked like the end for me was actually God leading me into the ministry he had for me all along. While I don't like what happened and would have preferred a different path, God used my illness for his glory."

PART VIII
HELP WHEN YOU CREATE TROUBLE

*Jesus spoke to those who had come—
high priests, Temple police, religion leaders:
"What is this, jumping me with swords
and clubs as if I were a dangerous criminal?
Day after day I've been with you in the Temple
and you've not so much as lifted a hand
against me. But do it your way—it's a dark
night, a dark hour." (Luke 22:52–54 MSG)*

*"When you say a situation or a person
is hopeless, you are slamming the door
in God's face" —Anonymous*

It's Not Too Late

A TEMPORARY LAPSE in good judgment cannot cancel the plans of God. Regardless what your emotions are telling you, life is far from over. When feeling overwhelmed it's easy to make bad decisions and do things you later regret. You're so much more than the mistakes you've made, doubts you've had, or worries you've given into.

Key Verse: "No sooner were the words out of his mouth than a crowd showed up, Judas, the one from the Twelve, in the lead. He came right up to Jesus to kiss him. Jesus said, 'Judas, you would betray the Son of Man with a kiss?'" (Luke 22:47–48 MSG).

When Judas led the mob to the Mount of Olives, he was creating more than a stir among his peers. He was conjuring up his own demise. He may or may not have realized the ramifications of what he was about to do. But one thing is certain, he made a terrible mistake.

I can see Judas, leading the dark to the Light. I can't help but wonder what he was thinking. Perhaps, the other disciples saw him coming and thought, *It's about time he showed up. We have been here for hours without him. Oh look, at least he brought some friends to help us pray.*

Jesus was right when he said, "But do it your way—it's a dark night, a dark hour" (Luke 22:52–54 MSG). Judas didn't just arrive late to a prayer meeting—that would have been easily overlooked by the Master. Even the disciples who did show up to pray, couldn't stay awake. In the same way, you've, no doubt, neglected your spiritual responsibilities at times. I have missed a prayer service or two, myself. This portion is about so much more than your occasional drifting from spiritual activity. Judas is proof you can stir up your own trouble even if you sit pew side every Sunday morning. Think about it. Jesus was Judas's pastor. The disciples were his brothers in arms. He was surrounded by the supernatural power of God and yet he still allowed poor choices to overtake him—proving there aren't enough chandeliers in all the sanctuaries of the world to extinguish the darkness you invite.

Judas may have been leading the pack but he would soon come in last. The blackest night is the one you create. I think mostly because it could have been avoided. Chaos and consequences are hard to swallow when you have no one but yourself to blame. Some might argue Judas was a backslider. I tend to believe he was more of a darkness inviter. The Scripture clearly points out he was the one from the "Twelve." While he no doubt had spiritual issues, he was still very much associated with the other eleven. Judas was conflicted. You don't have to cash in your church membership card to do something with long-term consequences. In fact, I know a lot of people who I truly believe love God, but like Judas, they got themselves involved in something, and they're having a hard time getting out. Perhaps, it was an affair or maybe a really bad decision that put them at odds with those they love. The cause isn't as important as the outcome. Once Jesus gets involved, it doesn't have to be, "A dark night, a dark hour."

Sadly, Judas believed a lie. Even though he was seized with remorse over his actions, he saw no path forward and hung himself (Matthew 27:5). The end of your rope doesn't have to leave you at the end of a rope. Matthew tells us why:

> "You're blessed when you're at the end of your rope. With less of you there is more of God and his rule." (Matthew 5:3 MSG)

It's not too late. Had Judas gone to Jesus seeking forgiveness and restoration, rather than going to the chief priest and elders, his story might have had a different ending. We will never know. Matthew had a bird's-eye view:

> When Judas, who had betrayed him, saw that Jesus was condemned, he was seized with remorse and returned the thirty pieces of silver to the chief priests and elders. "I have sinned," he said, "for I have betrayed innocent blood." (Matthew 27:3–4a)

Judas said all the right things to all the wrong people. He even admitted sinning. Satan may have heavily influenced him in the past, but at this point he was under conviction. I realize it can sometimes be hard to see past our bad choices and difficult to know who to approach in order to make them right. The pain and damage we've all, at times, inflicted upon others can seem beyond repair. Hopelessness abounds in our mistakes. If this is your current story, I only request you figuratively take my hand, put down the rope, and keep reading.

Reflection Journal: If you've invited the darkness (or at least contributed to it), write a letter to God expressing your willingness to correct your mistakes. Go to Jesus, not the chief priest.

_____

_____

_____

_____

_____

Fear Blocker

"Since, then, you have been raised with Christ, set your hearts on things above, where Christ is seated at the right hand of God. Set your mind on things above, not on earthly things. For you died and your life is now hidden in Christ in God" (Colossians 3:1–3).

■ ■ ■

You Don't Belong Here

DON'T CONFUSE WHO you are with what you sometimes do. Satan knows your name but calls you by your sin. God knows your sin but calls you by your name.

Key Verse: "You are all children of the light and children of the day. We do not belong to the night or to the darkness" (1 Thessalonians 5:5).

You've probably heard the phrase, "He made his bed, now he can lay in it." When I was a child my grandma used to say that to me if I did something to get in trouble, which was quite often. I think she meant, "Don't be mad at me for punishing you, after all, you're the one who misbehaved." While children (including God's children) do need discipline, we need not forget when the disciples entered the tomb, they found the bed of Jesus not only empty but made (John 20:6–8). Jesus made his bed so you wouldn't have to lie in yours.

Perhaps you've slipped into something shady. You know you don't belong there and you certainly didn't plan on an extended stay. What you thought you wanted wasn't as advertised. It just doesn't feel right. Satan wormed his way into your head and you're not yourself. This is not your crowd and this is not what you wanted, nonetheless, it's where you are. Does that resonate or can you remember a time when it did? Maybe, like

Pharaoh, your willful rejection of God's ways caused a plague of darkness so thick you can feel it (Exodus 10:21). Like Egypt, blackout has settled over your land.

While the darkness may belong to you, in that it has your fingerprints all over it, you do not belong to it. You have the power to decide when and if you overcome. Judas could have recovered and, like Peter after his denial, found an even deeper, more fulfilling relationship with Christ. At the end of his rope, Judas chose the end of a rope.

The anxiety created by bad decisions is on a mission to shake you down, and you may feel as if you deserve to go down. Will you use your rope to climb out of the dark and into the light of a new beginning? Will you allow your story to end with a glorious resurrection, rather than the gloominess of a casket full of mistakes? You don't have to die in the dark. You are not Judas.

Jesus wasn't just an expert on the light. He also had a thorough understanding of the dark and what can happen when you choose to walk in it. Jesus knew what was at stake. He spoke of it often to his disciples. Apparently, Judas was busy counting other people's money the day Jesus explained just how dangerous the dark path can be:

> Jesus said, "For a brief time still, the light is among you. Walk by the light you have so darkness doesn't destroy you. If you walk in darkness, you don't know where you're going. As you have the light, believe in the light. Then the light will be within you, and shining through your lives. You'll be children of light." (John 12:35–36 MSG)

Jesus makes a strong case. He plainly tells his followers the sole purpose of darkness is to cause their destruction. He portrays two paths with very different endings. You can walk in the light and the light will shine through you or you can walk in darkness and not know where you're going. Having spent countless hours with those who have created their own darkness, I can say with certainty most feel lost and without a sense of direction. The once well-lit path has become a dark, winding trail up the mountain side. Calm, cool, and collected becomes chaos, drama, and scattered when you choose to walk that dark path. Jesus nailed it when he said, "Walk by the light . . . so darkness doesn't destroy you."

Reflection Journal: What names does Satan sometimes call you? Today, tell him who you really are.

_____

_____

_____

_____

_____

Fear Blocker

"The LORD is my light and my salvation—whom shall I fear? The LORD is the stronghold of my life—of whom shall I be afraid?" (Psalm 27:1).

▩ ▩ ▩

There Is a Way Out

IF THE WALLS are closing in—climb out.

Key Verse: "The people walking in darkness have seen a great light" (Isaiah 9:2b).

As I child I loved to watch the show *Let's Make a Deal.* Basically, the premise was to offer a contestant something that may or may not have value. They could then trade it for something else or keep it for themselves. Again, they had no way of knowing if what they were trading for was better than what they had, as the value of either had not yet been revealed. Someone might hit the jackpot or lose it all depending on the trade. God is offering you a trade. Only he is not going to keep you in the suspense about the offer. Your troublesome thoughts can be exchanged for something better. God offers no gimmicks, hidden curtains, or mystery boxes. There are only three steps:

Step One: Come Out

> But you are a chosen people, a royal priesthood, a holy nation, God's special possession, that you may declare the praises of him who called you out of darkness into his wonderful light. (1 Peter 2:9)

As simple as it sounds, the only way out of a dark closet is to come out the same way you went in—through the door. There is no backdoor deal or slipping under the floorboards. It's a straightforward march into the light. Satan wants you to believe you're forever walled in after you've given up hope or, like Judas, possibly even done something ridiculous. At this point, I think it's important to mention that while sin does produce death, it also offers temporary pleasure (Hebrews 11:25). So the thought of coming out right now may not excite you. In fact, it would not surprise me to find out you're still resisting, because the darkness is providing you with some benefit.

Maybe you're like a friend of mine, who recently reached out to me. She was going through a very dark time she created all on her own and needed some advice. I told her she needed to turn away from what she was doing and turn toward Jesus. Her reply was, "I can't do that. I enjoy my life of sin." When this is the case, it's usually because the payback hasn't yet caught up to the payoff. If this is true for you, I am guessing you're apprehensive and still clinging to what could eventually take you down. Just like with Judas, Satan will be working hard to expertly blind you to the possibility of rescue. He might even be whispering, "You don't need to be rescued." His tactics must be refused.

A willingness to come out of the shadows is the first and most important step. Until you're ready to do this, be prepared for the continued fallout. If you're pushed into the light by circumstances, you will worm your way back into the dark. If you're pulled out into the light by someone else, you'll eventually find a way around them and return to the shadows. God won't drag you back to your senses; you must come back on your own. Seized with remorse, Judas made it to step one. Unfortunately, that is as far as he got.

Step Two: Be Delivered

> God rescued us from dead-end alleys and dark
> dungeons. He's set us up in the kingdom of the Son
> he loves so much, the Son who got us out of the pit
> we were in, got rid of the sins we were doomed to
> keep repeating. (Colossians 1:13–14 MSG)

Deliverance begins with repentance. God will burst through
the doors of your dungeon if you're willing to renounce what
put you there in the first place. While sin is a deliberate turning
from God, repentance is a deliberate turning to God. Blackout
always happens when you allow unchecked sinful behavior to
operate in your life on a repeated loop. When you live with your
foot on the rising sun, don't be surprised when life feels like
a never-ending night. John tells us what to do when we have
more nightmares than daydreams:

> This is the message we have heard from him and
> declare to you: God is light, in him there is no
> darkness at all. If we claim we have fellowship with
> him yet walk in darkness, we lie and do not live by
> the truth. But if we walk in the light, as he is in the
> light, we have fellowship with one another and the
> blood of Jesus, his Son, purifies us from all sin. If
> we claim to be without sin, we deceive ourselves
> and the truth is not in us. If we confess our sins, he
> is faithful and just and will forgive us our sins and
> purify us from all unrighteousness. (1 John 1:5–9)

You cannot skip this step. In your own words always be
willing to tell God exactly what you've done. The Faithful One

can handle your unfaithfulness. Don't be afraid to spill it all out and come completely clean. Admit it and own it. Do it now.

Step Three: Turn Away

> "To open their eyes and turn them from darkness to light, and from the power of Satan to God, so that they may receive forgiveness of sins and a place among those who are sanctified by faith in me." (Acts 26:18)

In the above verse, Paul the apostle is explaining the process of salvation to King Agrippa. Here, he talks about a deliberate turning from darkness to light. He, of all people, knew how important this step is. Paul was a shady character before he met Jesus. It was his willingness to turn away from the life he once knew that made the difference. Once you have decided to come out and have asked God to deliver you through forgiveness, now comes the most difficult part—you must turn away from whatever turned you away from the light.

Reflection Journal: Now that you've turned away from the dark, how will you stay away?

_____

_____

_____

_____

_____

Fear Blocker

"My guilt has overwhelmed me like a burden too heavy to bear. My wounds fester and are loathsome because of my sinful folly. I am bowed down and brought very low; all day long I go about mourning. My back is filled with searing pain; there is no health in my body. I am feeble and utterly crushed; I groan in anguish of heart. All my longings lie open before you, Lord; my sighing is not hidden from you" (Psalm 38:4–9).

■ ■ ■

Part VIII

Beacons of Light

- "But if we walk in the light, as he is in the light, we have fellowship with one another, and the blood of Jesus Christ his Son, purifies us from all sin" (1 John 1:7).

- "For you were once darkness, but now you are light in the Lord. Live as children of the light (for the fruit of the light consists in all goodness, righteousness, and truth) and find out what pleases the Lord. Have nothing to do with the fruitless deeds of darkness, but rather expose them" (Ephesians 5:8–11).

- "Therefore, if your whole body is full of light, and no part of it dark, it will be just as full of light as when a lamp shines its light on you" (Luke 11:36).

A Story of Unshakable Faith

Raised in a strong Southern Baptist family, the last thing Missy expected was to be a single mom at the age of twenty-one. Eventually, she met the man she believed God was saving for her. He was good looking, charming, and charismatic. He had a good job and was able to provide more than most. "It was easy for me to accept his offer of marriage. I not only loved him, I respected him. I felt like my life was finally on track," she said.

Not long after their wedding, her new husband had some friends over. They stayed late, so she excused herself and went to bed. Missy said, "I had just drifted off to sleep when I felt an arm reach around me. Thinking it was my husband, I rolled over. Instead, I saw the face of one of his friends. Before I could say a word, I noticed my husband standing in the doorway with a video camera." Over the next few months Missy continued to have sex with whomever her husband invited into their bedroom. She said, "I don't know why I did it or didn't tell anyone. I felt like I had just turned off the light switch and I didn't know how, or if, I could turn it back on. My life and everything in it went black."

As a result, Missy became pregnant and the baby did not belong to her husband. To complicate things further, her body was so badly damaged, the doctors weren't sure if she could safely deliver. She was also told future pregnancies were now impossible. Life began to spiral. After the birth of her son, her husband kicked her out. Missy fell apart. In the dark, without any sense of direction, she hopped on a bus leaving everything and everyone behind. Hundreds of miles from home, she tried starting over, but the darkness was too thick.

At rock bottom, she wanted to die. Suicide was now a real option. Afraid to die and afraid to live, she visited a church.

There she met a dear woman who took her in. Listen as Missy explains how her journey out of blackout began. "This precious lady was sent from God. She taught me that I didn't have to stay in the dark place that I had created. I could be forgiven and restored. What had happened to me was not beyond God's ability to forgive." Twenty years have passed and while Missy still occasionally struggles with what happened; she is happy, healthy, and living in the light of a new day.

PART IX
THE ODDS ARE IN YOUR FAVOR

Leaving there, they went through Galilee.
He didn't want anyone to know their
whereabouts, for he wanted to teach his
disciples. He told them, "The Son of Man is
about to be betrayed to some people who want
nothing to do with God. They will murder him.
Three days after his murder, he will rise, alive."
They didn't know what he was talking about,
but were afraid to ask him about it.
(Mark 9:30–32 MSG)

"Where there is no vision, there is no hope."
—George Washington Carver

You Can Lie Down in Green Pastures

IF THERE'S A Goliath in front of you, there is a King David inside you.

Key Verse: "He makes me lie down in green pastures, he leads me beside quiet waters" (Psalm 23:2).

I am not a sports guy. I do, however, on occasion watch the Super Bowl. Even then, I'll admit, I'm more interested in the snacks and what's going on behind the scenes than I am the game. I like chicken wings and the back-story—I want to know which team wasn't supposed to make it to the championship but somehow found a way and which players are over-performing. Just tell me who came out of the shadows and shined the brightest so I can put more jalapenos on my nachos! The underdogs get my vote. I always root for the team who silenced the naysayers and proved they had the hidden ability to get the job done—those who pushed back every worrisome thought of losing and found a way to rise.

When Jesus told his disciples he was going to be murdered and resurrected three days later, they were confused and upset. Their theology had no place for a suffering and dying Messiah (Mark 9:10). As of yet, there were no paintings of God on a cross, choirs singing he is risen, preachers shouting death couldn't hold him, or books written about his power over the grave. Not to mention the time factor. With each passing hour in the tomb, the odds of resurrection were less likely. This only complicated the situation, making those closest to Jesus nervous.

From the time Jesus died until he came out of the grave alive, there was a gap in time. Blackout can happen in this "gap." This chasm of despair, could also be described as those moments in life where the odds aren't encouraging. In fact, they might even be disappointing. With each passing minute, the disciples believed the gap was getting wider—expanding the darkness—and shoving out the light. In reality, the chasm was closing, pushing out the darkness as Jesus moved toward the light of an Easter sunrise.

In this "gap" the odds won't seem in your favor. How you react, when it looks like there is more against you than for you, is crucial. Here, you will be tempted to give up. Perception will always overrule reality when you look at the odds through the lens of why you feel outmatched. You must forget the odds and refuse to concentrate on who or what murdered you.

The destination isn't where you've been or even where you currently are. The destination is where you're going. The "gap" can make you restless or it can be a rest stop along the way. You can lie down in defeat or you can lie down in green pastures (Psalm 23:2). The enemy knows the odds and he is betting against you. Make him regret placing that bet.

There are many examples in the Scriptures of those who spent time in the tomb of uncertainty—facing astronomical odds stacked against them. Jesus wasn't the only one to find himself in a dark cave, waiting on God to breathe life into what others might consider a hopeless situation. When life blacks out, the chasm you're in often feels like the Grand Canyon. It can be scary when you can't see across to the other side and have no idea how long it will take to get out. The steep rock walls feel like a prison as you move your hands along the rough stone enclosure. Abraham knew this all too well, however, this founding father of Israel defied the odds. And so can you:

> When everything was hopeless, Abraham believed anyway, deciding to live, not on the basis of what he saw he couldn't do, but on what God said he would do. And so he was made father of a multitude of peoples. God himself said to him, "You're going to have a big family, Abraham!" (Romans 4:18 MSG)

What are the chances of a one-hundred-year-old man and a ninety-year-old woman conceiving and giving birth to a son (Genesis 21:5)? No wonder Sarah laughed when the angel told her Isaac was in her future. She even said, "An old woman like me? Get pregnant? With this old man of a husband?" (Genesis 18:12 MSG). The conception of Isaac was just as funny to her as it is to us. Imagine if your grandparents approached you to help paint their nursery! You might have some questions. The odds weren't a million to one. The odds were impossible. Even with modern medical advancement, the oldest woman believed to have given birth in recent times is a seventy-four-year-old Spanish woman.

Not even the shadiest bookie would have tried to get bets placed on Abraham's hopeless situation. After all, who in their right mind would roll the dice on something so impossible? God would. When you can call the things that are not as though they are (Romans 4:17), you don't consult the odds makers. You don't sit up at night worrying about the details or playing "what if." During blackout, it can be impossible to see the arrival of what you've been promised. And in this case, I am willing to go out on a limb and say not only could Abraham and Sarah not see the promise; everything—including their bodies—were in contradiction to that promise. When life contradicts God's promises, that's not the time to allow your stress levels to overwhelm you, because at that moment you're close to birthing a miracle.

I think it's important to note Abraham was eighty-five years old when the promise of Isaac first came (Genesis 15:4). With each passing year, the gap between the promise and the answer became wider and the odds grew worse. I'm not much of a gambler. In fact, I've never even been to a casino, but I do know the worse the odds, the bigger the payoff. That tells me if you've been in the dark for a long period of time, with more working against you than for you, get ready to hit the jackpot!

Reflection Journal: Impossible odds bring improbable results when, like Abraham, you decide to believe anyway. Make a list of what seems impossible—now, place your bet on God!

Fear Blocker

"I know what it is like to be in need, and I know what it is like to have plenty. I have learned the secret of being content in any and every situation, whether well fed or hungry, whether living in plenty or in want. I can do all things through him who strengthens me" (Philippians 4:12–13 ESV).

■ ■ ■

The Odds Against You Are Never Greater Than the God Beside You

TRYING TO OUTRUN God never works to your advantage. Today, allow God's plan to come together.

Key Verse: "Abraham didn't focus on his own impotence and say, 'It's hopeless. This hundred-year-old body could never father a child.' Nor did he survey Sarah's decades of infertility and give up. He didn't tiptoe around God's promise asking cautiously skeptical questions. He plunged into the promise and came up strong, ready for God, sure that God would make good on what he had said" (Romans 4:19–22 MSG).

Satan is working to pull your expectations for the future down to what you're currently experiencing. One of his chief tactics is to fool you into believing you've canceled what God has up his sleeve—all because of some alternative methods you tried when anxiety over the future was pressing hard against you. The solutions we come up with on our own always backfire and can become the source of our agitation. Before Abraham trusted God to make good on what he said, he made some very real mistakes. In his attempt to solve his own problem, he did something dumb:

> Sarai, Abram's wife, hadn't yet produced a child. She had an Egyptian maid named Hagar. Sarai said to Abram, "GOD has not seen fit to let me have a child. Sleep with my maid. Maybe I can get a family from her." Abram agreed to do what Sarai said. (Genesis 16:1–2 MSG)

Instead of calming their minds by waiting on God's perfect timing, Abraham and Sarah only added to their stress level by trying to speed up the process with their own solution. Their impatience with the Lord's failure to give them what they wanted only contributed to an already chaotic situation. An angel of the Lord gave this message to Hagar:

> "From this pregnancy, you'll get a son: Name him Ishmael; for GOD heard you, GOD answered you. He'll be a bucking bronco of a man, a real fighter, fighting and being fought, always stirring up trouble, always at odds with his family." (Genesis 16:11–12 MSG)

From that day forward Sarah began mistreating Hagar. Having taken all the abuse she could stand, Hagar fled.

Before Abraham received what God told him was coming, he received a bucking, fighting, troublemaker. Anytime you step away from the purposes of God, you can expect some backlash. God in his sovereignty will not approve of your departure from the truth, nor will he bless the arrogant dismissal of his word. Thankfully, God is also merciful. Abraham's mistake didn't affect the final outcome. It did, however, make his life more complicated while waiting for Isaac. You never increase the odds by taking matters into your own hands. Doing so will only add to your level of uneasiness.

If you have birthed an Ishmael while waiting for an Isaac, it can still be okay. Like Abraham, sometimes we are forced to raise a "problem" child alongside the "promised" child. God did not withhold Isaac due to the poor choices of Abraham and Sarah, and God will not withhold what he has promised you because of a bad decision or two.

If you're like me, you have gotten ahead of God on more than one occasion. On my own, I have tried to make the impossible, possible. As a result, I have changed Ishmael's diapers. Doing things my way hasn't ever gotten me anywhere worth going. The problem with running ahead of God is he is never allowed to catch up. Also, it's impossible to see where you're going when the light is behind you. When I slow down and stop trying to manipulate the situation, God not only matches my stride, he carries me in his arms. The odds are only against you when you try to do life your way.

Reflection Journal: Has stress been pushing you to do things your way and in your timing? How will you slow down so God can catch up?

_____

_____

_____

Fear Blocker:

"For nothing will be impossible with God" (Luke 1:37 ESV).

■ ■ ■

The Ingredients for a Miracle

MIRACLES HAPPEN WHEN circumstances are beyond human repair. Today, offer God the tattered pieces of what would be impossible for you to repair without his help.

Key Verse: "But it's not just Abraham; it's also us! The same thing gets said about us when we embrace and believe the One who brought Jesus to life when the conditions were equally hopeless" (Romans 4:24 MSG).

Crushed, pierced, stricken, and wounded (Isaiah 53) aren't the usual ingredients for a miracle. Jesus's body was in no condition to be resurrected. He didn't just die. He was beaten beyond recognition. Resurrection also meant the restoration of that which was whipped, stripped, and torn. The knots in your stomach can turn into a belly full of laughs.

Resurrection and restoration aren't the same and yet, they go together. Resurrection is when God breathes life into that which is considered dead, while restoration is when God puts something back together. God not only raised Jesus back to life, he also put the bruised body of Jesus back together. In the same way, anytime your life falls apart, God will mend every broken place if you'll embrace and believe in him. Your life will never be beyond God's repair, no matter how tattered or tangled.

Allow the same hands that closed the wounded side of Jesus to close your wounds. Relax, knowing the same God who stitched up the back of Jesus, has your back. Your tomb can become an emergency room when you understand God operates best when things look darkest.

How you view the future will have a profound impact upon the direction your life will take. If you believe the odds against you are too great, they are. If you believe the odds don't really matter because God is too great, they don't. This book is laced with stories of people just like you who weren't supposed to make it but they did, because they had a positive expectation and vision for the future. They decided what looked like the end—wasn't the end.

If the enemy can take away your hope for a good life, you will always be stuck in the gloom of your current crisis. If you want to come out of the dark, bathe in the light, and walk in the promises of a better tomorrow, there is only one way. Your hope must be pointed in the direction God is leading you. Allow your expectation level to rise and believe God for the impossible. The future hasn't yet met the problems of your past. Make sure they never meet by refusing to introduce them.

Reflection Journal: All Jesus had to offer God after blackout was brokenness and more brokenness. What still hurts and how will you invite God into whatever ingredients you have left?

Fear Blocker

"For I am the LORD your God who takes hold of your right hand and says to you, Do not fear; I will help you" (Isaiah 41:13).

❚ ❚ ❚

Part IX

Beacons of Light

- "You, LORD, keep my lamp burning; my God turns my darkness into light. With your help I can advance against a troop; with my God I can scale a wall" (Psalm 18:28–29).

- "Light, space, zest—that's GOD! So, with him on my side I am fearless, afraid of no one and nothing. When vandal hordes ride down ready to eat me alive, those bullies and toughs fall flat on their faces. When besieged, I'm calm as a baby. When all hell breaks loose, I'm collected and cool" (Psalm 27:1–3 MSG).

- "I saw that wisdom is better than folly, just as light is better than darkness" (Ecclesiastes 2:13).

A Story of Unshakable Faith

The Anthonys were a typical family. Gary and Susan married and had two daughters: Mikalyn and Hailey. When Susan became pregnant with baby number three, they had no idea what was coming or the amount of faith it would take to get them through it. Macy was born at twenty-eight weeks. At first the doctors were hopeful, not knowing she wasn't just premature. It quickly became evident something else was wrong with Macy. After a more thorough examination, she was diagnosed with 22Q11.2 microduplication. "The doctors told us there are only sixty known cases worldwide and Macy is the only surviving preemie. They gave us no hope and began preparing us for the worst," Susan explained.

After two weeks, the hospital requested an ethics meeting with the Anthonys. The doctors insisted keeping Macy alive was unethical and that they should remove all means of life support. This would mean instant death as Macy's lungs were not yet developed enough to breathe on her own. "They instructed us on how to plan the day of her death. Even suggesting that we could pass her dead body around the room, allowing everyone the opportunity to say goodbye but we weren't ready to let her go. We knew that God could save Macy and that if he wanted her to live, she deserved the chance to fight," Susan said.

The Anthonys refused the doctors' advice, choosing instead to put their hope and trust in God. The next month wasn't easy. Macy's heart even stopped fourteen times in one day. Gary and Susan continued to place Macy in God's hand. One month later the hospital sent Macy home to die but she did not die. In fact, she continued to improve. Defying all odds, Macy lived to be five years old. Macy sat beside me as her mom shared this story of hope just a few months before Macy went home to be with Jesus. The Anthonys left me with this thought. "We did have doubts and thought more than once maybe we wouldn't have any time at all with her. We trusted God anyway and knew that when God was ready for Macy, he would take her. Until then, she got to stay with us!"

PART X
YOU CAN GET OVER WHATEVER TOOK YOU UNDER

*"Like Jonah, three days and nights
in the fish's belly, the Son of Man will be
gone three days and nights in a deep grave."
(Matthew 12:40 MSG)*

*"In trouble, deep trouble, I prayed to God.
He answered me. From the belly of the grave
I cried, 'Help!' You heard my cry." —Jonah*

I Didn't Expect This

IN THE MIDDLE of a violent squall (Jonah 1:4), God sent Jonah's ride. No yacht, jet ski, or water patrol in this story—just the rumbling belly of a giant sea monster. There probably wasn't even good internet service.

Key Verse: "Now the LORD provided a huge fish to swallow Jonah, and Jonah was in the belly of the fish three day and three nights" (Jonah 1:17).

I love the story of Jonah and the great fish. You have to admit as far as fish stories go, this one is a whopper! You don't hear about a fish that caught a man. I was five years old the first time I heard about Jonah and his encounter with what could only be described as a giant sea beast. I remember sitting wide-eyed as the Sunday school teacher, Mrs. Bohannon, stood in front of the class using a felt board and figures cut out of cloth to explain what happened. (If you're over the age of forty and grew up in church, you know exactly what I'm talking about.)

She placed the water first, then a boat full of sailors. Next, a scuffle broke out. Jonah was blamed for the storm and thrown overboard by his shipmates. I moved closer to the edge of my seat when I saw the great fish in her hand. What was going to happen? Surely the fish would push Jonah to the shore or perhaps even gently lift him back into the boat. After all, he was

a preacher who just had a conversation with God. To my surprise, the fish did not rescue him, the fish swallowed him. That's
right. Instead of God taking Jonah over the storm, the fish took
him under it (Jonah 1:1–17). What if the way over is under?
Would that calm you?

Occasionally in life, the last thing you expect to happen
will happen. You've been paying the electric bill faithfully every
month but with no explanation, the lights went out anyway.
Even though Jonah wasn't acting in complete obedience to the
Lord at the time, I bet he never even considered being swallowed by a fish. In fact, the thought probably never crossed his
mind. We know right before he became fish food, he was sleep-
ing comfortably below the deck of the ship (Jonah 1:5). Even
after he was thrown overboard, I'm sure sea monsters weren't
on his radar. Drowning, maybe? Getting struck by lightning?
That could happen. Being swallowed by a fish? No way.

No wonder Jesus used this legendary story from the Old
Testament to describe to the Pharisees what was going to actually take place once he was swallowed by the grave. They knew
the story of Jonah and what a miracle it was for him to have
survived what should have easily killed him. Even though Jesus
would die from the injuries he sustained at the cross, he too
went on a three-day journey into the deep unknown.

Like the great fish, the tomb was Jesus's ride. It's usually not
a limousine carrying you past what keeps you up at night. The
limelight has never taken me very far. Don't call the coast guard
when the giant fish swims up. Like Jesus, allow the blackout
you're experiencing to carry you into the light of what God
intended all along. The method of transportation isn't nearly as
important as the final destination.

Remember, you cannot conquer kingdoms if you never face enemies, and shutting the mouths of lions is impossible if you only pet kittens. Flames aren't quenched while you're warming yourself beside comfortable fires, and the dead are never raised if nothing ever dies.

I realize while blackout can feel like punishment, that is not always the case. As we have discussed in previous days, sometimes that happens and, apparently, was true for Jonah (Jonah 1:3). Jesus, however, was completely innocent when the grave swallowed him. You're probably somewhere in the middle. Maybe you're not running from God but you're not necessarily running toward him with all you've got. The giant fish swallowed you, put you in the dark, and is swimming circles. Dizzy, you sit there wondering how you will ever get over what took you under.

Reflection Journal: Describe how Jonah must have felt while in the belly of the fish. Now, compare that with how you feel and explain what you'll do to keep going.

Fear Blocker

"So do not fear, for I am with you; do not be dismayed, for I am your God. I will strengthen you and help you; I will uphold you with my righteous right hand" (Isaiah 41:10).

▩ ▩ ▩

Fish Prayers

LIKE A FIRST responder, God was first to respond to Jonah's S.O.S. Your prayers aren't just going up, they're going into listening ears—God's ears.

Key Verse: "From inside the fish Jonah prayed to the LORD his God" (Jonah 2:1).

Jonah didn't wait for even the smallest flicker of light before he began seeking the Light. The conditions he found himself in weren't conducive to your typical prayer service. There were no altars, communion trays, or even soft music to set the mood. His problems wrapped him tighter than seaweed ever could. Incarcerated behind the rib cage of the great fish, Jonah cried out for help. All alone and under an ocean of trouble, he began seeking the Lord.

There is just something about the cry of a child coming from a dark place a dad can't ignore. When my sons were toddlers, neither required much sleep. This created a real problem for my wife and me as our need for rest only increased after they came along. Bedtime was rough at our house. All the books we read suggested the best thing you can do for a sleepless child is not to go into their room at night, even if they're crying. Apparently, this sends a signal of rescue, teaching them to cry instead of calming themselves down and going back to sleep on their own. I will confess, I couldn't do it. I found it impossible to ignore those little voices crying, "Daddy." As a result, I slept many nights on the floor with a toddler playing by my side. I broke all the rules of parenting, but for me it was the best choice. Now my sons are grown men, I cherish those memories. Rescuing them from the dark gave me peace of mind and gave them the security of knowing Dad was just a sniffle away.

God is your Father (Matthew 6:9). He cannot hold himself back while one of his children is crying. The need to find and rescue you supersedes the notion you can calm down on your own. Tears, like coordinates on a map, draw him to your side. If you're waiting for conditions to improve before you cry out, you've already waited too long. From the inside of the fish, Jonah prayed:

> "When my life was slipping away, I remembered God, and my prayer got through to you, made it all the way to your Holy Temple." (Jonah 2:7 MSG)

Reflection Journal: Take a look around. What do you see? Pray a fish prayer.

_____

_____

_____

_____

_____

Fear Blocker:

"Let the peace of Christ rule in your hearts, since as members of one body you were called to peace" (Colossians 3:15).

※ ※ ※

*God Can Speak to What
Has Swallowed You*

GOD TOOK JONAH and Jesus over what took them under.
He will do the same for you.

Key Verse: "Then GOD spoke to the fish, and it vomited up
Jonah on the seashore" (Jonah 2:10 MSG).

Overwhelmed and in the throes of despair, Jonah was
honest and vulnerable with God. His prayer was authentic
(Jonah 2:1–10). Religious etiquette flies out the window when
life swallows you. Jonah's life may have been slipping, but
God's ability to speak to his capture never slipped. God still
speaks to the fish (problems) that gulp you down. Your prayers
get through. Like shafts of light cutting through the blackest
night, your cries find God's ears. He will take you over what
took you under.

I think it's interesting that while Jonah was swallowed by a
fish, Jesus cooked fish for his disciples after his resurrection. I
love the story of breakfast with Jesus, as told by John. It's one
of my favorites. It's a typical fishing story. The followers of Jesus
had been casting their nets all night but caught nothing (John
21:3). I think they were fishing in some of my spots! As the sun

was coming up, the worn-out group spots Jesus on the shore, and he pokes a little fun at them, asking if they caught anything (John 21:5). Of course, he already knew the answer was no. Fishermen aren't always known for being truthful about their catch. I think Jesus asked with a grin his disciples couldn't see:

> When they landed, they saw a fire of burning coals there with fish on it, and some bread. (John 21:9)

This story proves Jesus can take what swallowed you and serve it back to you as a delicious meal. Garnish it with praise (Jonah 2:9)! Pepper it with thanksgiving! A tragic dilemma becomes a candlelit dinner with Jesus when you cry out from inside the fish.

The psalmist David knew the dark places of life are where God shines brightest. He offers this bit of advice when life goes off the rails of restlessness:

> Help, GOD—I've hit rock bottom! Master, hear my cry for help! Listen hard! Open your ears! Listen to my cries for mercy. . . . I pray to GOD—my life a prayer—and wait for what he'll say and do. My life's on the line before God, my Lord, waiting and watching till morning, waiting and watching till morning. (Psalm 130:1–2, 5–6 MSG)

Reflection Journal: How is God speaking to your problems? What do you see him doing?

_____

_____

_____

_____

_____

Fear Blocker

"The fear of man lays a snare, but whoever trusts in the LORD is safe" (Proverbs 29:25 ESV).

■ ▨ ▤

Part X

Beacons of Light

- "For as long as I am in the world, there is plenty of light. I am the world's Light" (John 9:5 MSG).

- "The city does not need the sun or moon to shine on it, for the glory of God gives it light, and the Lamb is its lamp" (Revelation 21:23).

- "But whoever lives by the truth comes into the light, so that it may be seen plainly that what they have done has been done in the sight of God" (John 3:21).

A Story of Unshakable Faith

Motherhood was always important to Emily. Even as a little girl, being a mom was on the top of her "life goals" list. After she met and married Ed, she quickly began asking God for a son—and not just any son. She said, "I prayed for a blond-headed, brown-eyed baby boy, and that is exactly who God gave me." She named him Ethan. Not long after Ethan was born, her marriage fell apart and without warning, Ed packed up and left, taking Ethan with him. "In the '80s, it wasn't as easy to find someone as it is now days. In the beginning, I panicked. I had no idea where they had gone or if they would ever return," she said. Her worst fears were confirmed as Ed never came home. At the time, Emily had no way of knowing it would be almost two decades before she saw Ethan again.

At age twenty, Ethan tracked down his mom, moved back home, and they reconnected. She found out Ed was an abusive drunk to the boy as he was growing up, even allowing him to be put in situations of brutal harm. She also discovered Ethan grew into a good man, quite the opposite of his father. He loved God and avidly studied the Bible. Five years after moving back to Emily's home, Ethan began to feel a burden for his father. His dad was lost and without Christ. To everyone's surprise, he moved back to the city where his father lived and shared Jesus with Ed. Three weeks later on December 12th Emily received this Christmas card message from Ethan:

> Mom,
>
>   I hope you all have a wonderful Christmas. I miss you very much.
>
>   "Very truly I tell you, whoever obeys my word will never see death" (John 8:51).
>
>   I love you, Ethan

Seven days later on December 19th Ethan died from an accidental overdose. They buried him the day after Christmas. Emily gave Ed his Bible. She left me with this thought: "I am so grateful that God gave me a visible sign of hope. He really does care about his children. I could not have endured Ethan's death if it weren't for that Christmas card. I keep it in my Bible. When I look at it, I am reminded that death is not the end. I will see Ethan again very soon."

Hope took Emily over what took her under. She found out firsthand how important it is to cry out to God in the dark. Her willingness to turn toward God, rather than away from God during the unexpected, is what delivered her.

PART XI
DON'T LISTEN TO THEM

*Those who passed by hurled insults at him,
shaking their heads and saying, "You who are
going to destroy the temple and build it
in three days, save yourself! Come down
from the cross, if you are the Son of God!" In
the same way the chief priests, the teachers of
the law and the elders mocked him. "He saved
others," they said, "but he can't save himself!
He's the king of Israel! Let him come down
now from the cross, and we will believe in
him. He trusts in God. Let God rescue him . . ."
(Matthew 27:39–43a)*

*"You will never reach your destination if you
stop and throw stones at every dog that barks."
—Sir Winston Churchill*

What They Say Isn't Nearly as Important as What God Says

GOD WILL TAKE what the enemy meant to destroy you and use it as a catapult to launch you into the life you've always wanted. Today, tell the enemy you're not bothered by his opinion.

Key Verse: "They stripped him and put a scarlet robe on him, and twisted together a crown of thorns and set it on his head. They put a staff in his right hand and knelt down in front of him and mocked him. 'Hail, king of the Jews!' they said. They spit on him, and took the staff and struck him on the head again and again. After they had mocked him, they took off the robe and put his own clothes on him. Then they lead him away to crucify him" (Matthew 27:28–31).

Can you imagine going to a funeral and instead of hearing a well-written eulogy piled high with praise and accolades, all you heard were those in the crowd mocking and shouting insults at the one being buried? What if, instead of sharing stories about the life of the deceased or retelling the good deeds they did, the person officiating said, "He talked a lot about God but apparently God was unwilling to save him." As ridiculous as that may sound, it's what happened to Jesus. Even though Jesus wasn't dead yet, he did have a few last words spoken over him. When life got tough, Jesus could have used some encouragement—a reassuring voice to calm his fears and steady his nerves. The disciples may have quietly mourned him but the chief priest and teachers of the law openly mocked him. Even before he was nailed to the cross, the Romans offered more of the same.

When life hurts and you need to be encouraged, don't be surprised when those around you hurl insults, even if you're completely innocent. After a lashing, usually comes a tongue lashing. Satan will make sure of it. His intention is to keep you trapped in the shadows by conning you into believing you deserve to stay there. Even though Jesus was without fault, the enemy used scorn and ridicule to try and break his spirit. Jesus, however, refused to be broken. The taunting may have penetrated his ears but it never penetrated his heart. Over the next few days, we are going to look at how Jesus responded to those who offered only insults and criticism. Like Job, Jesus had miserable comforters in his time of need. Maybe you can relate:

> Then Job defended himself: "I've had all I can take of your talk. What a bunch of miserable comforters! Is there no end to your windbag speeches? What's your problem that you go on and on like this? If you were in my shoes, I could talk just like you. I could put together a terrific tirade and really let you have it. But I'd never do that. I'd console and comfort, make things better, not worse!" (Job 16:1–5 MSG)

Before resurrection, expect some ridicule. One thing is certain, Jesus did not deserve the treatment he received from the crowd. There is no record of anyone shouting compliments in his direction as he paid the ultimate price for the sins of the world and there was no cheerleading squad to help him push through the dark chasm of torture. It was exactly the opposite. I have a suspicion many who were spewing venom at him that day were some of the very ones he performed miracles for in the past. In all probability, mouths filled with the very fish and bread he provided were now filled with cheap shots and libel. Can you relate? You were there when they needed you, but now when you are upset, they have turned on you. Life has taught me those who are quick to jump on the bandwagon are generally the first to leap off. Either directly or indirectly, Jesus impacted all who were demanding his death.

Jesus was guilty of nothing. The psalmist offers this advice concerning what others sometimes say:

> Remember your word to your servant, for you have given me hope. My comfort in my suffering is this: Your promise preserves my life. The arrogant mock me without restraint, but I do not turn away from your law. I remember, Lord, your ancient laws, and I find comfort in them. (Psalm 119:49–51)

Even if everyone is letting you have it, causing your mind to spin like a tilt-a-whirl, the remedy is still the law of the Lord. The amount of time you spend without answers, in part, will be determined by how you react to those causing you pain. You can rise above those who would love to see you go down in flames. I am proof there is hope when others hurl insults.

Reflection Journal: How will you respond to those who hurl insults at you? What will you do in order to keep a good attitude?

_____

_____

_____

_____

_____

Fear Blocker

"Be still before the LORD and wait patiently for him; do not fret when people succeed in their ways, when they carry out their wicked schemes. Refrain from anger and turn away from wrath; do not fret—it only leads to evil. For those who are evil will be destroyed, but those who hope in the LORD will inherit the land" (Psalm 37:7–9).

❋ ❋ ❋

Never Trade Insult for Insult

EVEN BEFORE JESUS was crucified, he refused to engage in verbal squabbles with his critics. He did not toss back at them what they were throwing his way.

Key Verse: "Then the high priest stood up and said to Jesus, 'Are you not going to answer? What is this testimony that these men are bringing against you?' But Jesus remained silent" (Matthew 26:62).

While early in his ministry, Jesus did tell the Pharisees the truth about the condition of their hearts (Matthew 23:27), we have no record of Jesus trading verbal punches with them or anyone else, for that matter, during his crucifixion. It's hard for me to imagine the amount of restraint it took for Jesus not to fire back. Holding my tongue, especially when I'm weighed down in despair, has never been my strongest attribute. When God hugs me it's usually so he can slip one hand over my mouth! I am afraid I would have said, "Keep talking. It won't be long until I'm back from the grave and once I am back, I will be sending you there permanently!" It's a good thing the fate of the world wasn't on my shoulders that day.

Anxiety over what others say about us only escalates our need for self-vindication. It's one thing to ignore our critics when life is sunshine and roses, it's another thing when life is darkness and thorns. Jesus was able to shrug off what should have set him off. Like Solomon said:

> Fools have short fuses and explode all too quickly; the prudent quietly shrug off insults. (Proverbs 12:16 MSG)

You can loudly engage with those who point out all the reasons for your worries or, like Jesus, you can quietly ignore them. Both responses will have a profound impact on the outcome. The reward for holding your tongue far exceeds the temporary pleasure of venting on those who insult you. Giving them a piece of your mind will never bring peace to your mind. Jesus could have closed the mouths of his accusers; instead, he chose to keep his own mouth closed—and so can you. The writer of Romans says:

> Do not repay anyone evil for evil. Be careful to do what is right in the eyes of everyone. If it is possible, as far as it depends on you, live at peace with everyone. Do not take revenge, my friends, but leave room for God's wrath, for it is written: "It is mine to avenge; I will repay," says the Lord. On the contrary: "If your enemy is hungry, feed him; if he is thirsty, give him something to drink. In doing this, you will heap burning coals on his head." Do not be overcome by evil, but overcome evil with good. (Romans 12:17–21)

Trading insults in the dark leaves no room for God to reward you in the light. Take note of how Jesus handled his hecklers. What he refused to say, shouted louder than what he wanted to say. His accusers said it best: "He trusts in God. Let God rescue him . . ." (Matthew 27:43a).

The passersby were quick to bring up the past—even taunting Jesus with what he previously said about rebuilding the temple in three days (Matthew 27:40). The point being, before the nails split his wrists, before the sun refused to shine, Jesus made a lot of statements others deemed outrageous. The cross was his opportunity to trust God by "putting his money where his mouth had been." Knowing the future and doing what it takes to get there are not the same (especially when others are trying to sow seeds of doubt in your mind). Jesus made a lot of promises concerning what would happen at the cross. Now he would have to make due with them by tuning out all the negative noise and staying focused on the mission. It's easier to hear God speak when you're not distracted by the droning of the crowd.

Sometimes this is the case with us. We said all the right things when life was moving forward and the future clear. Others listened as we talked about what we would do if the temple were ever torn down. It's easy to stand in confidence when you don't have to rely on God for much. Trusting God for money to buy a single light bulb isn't quite the same as trusting God for money to pay the electric bill. Once the lights are out, the onlookers won't be far behind.

When others tear you down, you don't have to stay down either. Like Jesus, you can make a glorious comeback. Your hope isn't in your ability to rise above the insults of the crowd, your hope rests in his ability to carry you above those insults. Jesus held his tongue to encourage you to hold yours. Paul explains why:

> May our Lord Jesus Christ himself and God our
> Father, who loved us and by his grace gave us

eternal encouragement and good hope, encourage
your hearts and strengthen you in every good deed
and word. (2 Thessalonians 2:16–17)

Did you catch that? Jesus offers you eternal encouragement and good hope! We have hope, not because of who we
are but because of who he is. Others hurl insults. Jesus hurls
hope. Mountains of it! Hope piled high and easily accessible.
Because Jesus was willing to be insulted in the dark, you can be
encouraged in the dark. I bet you thought I was going to say, "in
the light," didn't you? The truth is, you don't need much encouragement when things are shining bright. The dark is where you
need a reassuring voice—God's voice.

Reflection Journal: Have you been trading insult for insult?
How will you stop?

Fear Blocker

"So we can confidently say, 'The Lord is my helper; I will not
fear; what can man do to me?'" (Hebrews 13:6 ESV).

■ ■ ■

Choose Forgiveness

FORGIVING THOSE WHO heap trouble on you will be impossible under your own strength. Today, Jesus offers you his strength. Take it.

Key Verse: "In the same way the robbers who were crucified with him also heaped insults on him" (Matthew 27:44).

Jesus wasn't the only one being crucified in Jerusalem that day. There were two others. Their crimes aren't explained; they're only described as robbers or thieves. We don't know who their parents were or what kind of struggles may have put them in a position to steal. To me the criminals have always been faceless characters whose only real purpose was to balance out hillside paintings of the crucifixion by providing two additional crosses. To Jesus, they were the reason for the crucifixion. These self-admitted sinners (Luke 23:41) hung just a few feet away from the Master. They were close enough to have a conversation with the Lord and one of them wasn't just casually offering an insult or two. He was heaping insults upon him.

The comments coming from the crowd and the mockery of the Roman soldiers would have been enough, but it didn't end there. One who was close enough to have Jesus's ear, piled on the criticism as well. As far as I'm concerned, this would have been a good time for Jesus to demonstrate his power. With the nod of his head, he could have stopped the beating heart of the worthless criminal and no one would have been the wiser. Instead, Jesus did something unusual when the other crucified robber made a final request:

> Then he said, "Jesus, remember me when you come into your kingdom." Jesus answered him, "Truly I tell you, today you will be with me in paradise." (Luke 23:42–43)

Most would have said, "Are you joking? You want me to remember you? How about I remember all the things you did to land here?" Not Jesus. Forgiveness is his nature. Murderers, thieves, adulterers, and sharp-tongued insulters all get mercy. Jesus never asked the thief to undo what he did with his life. He only promised to hold back death and secure his place in eternity. If you're waiting for the person who hurt you to take it back before you forgive them, you might never get the chance. Why not give yourself the gift of releasing the bitterness that accumulated when the offenses were flying? Forgiveness is a choice, your choice.

Jesus set the example. You can remember all the negative things that spilled out or like Jesus, you can allow forgiveness to spill out. This will not be easy. After all, Jesus died for those who insulted him and you're probably trying to figure out the best way to avoid killing those who have insulted you. King Solomon shares this wisdom:

> Do not say, "I'll pay you back for this wrong!"
> Wait for the LORD, and he will avenge you."
> (Proverbs 20:22)

Have you said, "I'll get you for this?" Vengeance is God's prerogative. If someone needs "getting," God will get them far better than you ever could. When you take matters into your own hands, you take them out of God's hands. Jesus saw the thief on the cross not as a threat but as a dying man who needed rescue. I remember hearing Joyce Meyer say, "Hurting people hurt people." She was right. The repentant thief proves those who fling the most mud are usually those stuck in the deepest ditch. Instead of paying him back for what he said, Jesus reached out to him and God delivered them both.

Maybe your critics are opportunities in disguise. Perhaps those with the biggest mouths hold your greatest potential. God doesn't promote you based upon your ability to walk with friends. How you walk with your enemies is a better indicator of where God is willing to take you. Paying others back isn't nearly as effective as helping people up, even when they're responsible for pushing you down. Solomon also said this: "Do not pay attention to every word people say" (Ecclesiastes 7:21a).

Sir Winston Churchill famously said, "You will never reach your destination if you stop and throw stones at every dog that barks." At the cross, the dogs were barking. Jesus could have taken the time to throw rocks at each of them. He chose a different route. He refused to allow negative chatter to sway him. The chief priest, elders, crowd members, and thieves were all trying to goad him into a response. Love was his response. His silence was louder than the crowd that day.

Reflection Journal: Make a list of those you need to forgive. Start by praying for each of them.

Fear Blocker

"The Lᴏʀᴅ himself goes before you and will be with you; he will never leave you or forsake you. Do not be afraid; do not be discouraged" (Deuteronomy 31:8).

❖ ❖ ❖

Part XI

Beacons of Light

- "In the same way, let your light shine before others, that they may see your good deeds and glorify your Father in heaven" (Matthew 5:16).

- "Here's another way to put it: You're here to be light, bringing out the God-colors in the world" (Matthew 5:14 ᴍsɢ).

- "There once was a man, his name John, sent by God to point out the way to the Life-Light. He came to show everyone where to look, who to believe in" (John 1:6–7 MSG).

A Story of Unshakable Faith

This is my story: By the time I was thirty-six years old, I surpassed most of my peers in ministry and was nearing the finish line on a five-million-dollar building program. The church I was pastoring was rapidly growing and in the top 1 percent of attendance in the United States. On the surface, everything seemed great. However, I was leading on empty. Marriage problems, combined with the stress of building a new facility, took me into a deep spiral of depression. I was very much trapped in the dark and yet at the same time, proclaiming the Light. I kept it well hidden, and no one was aware of what was silently happening to me.

Burned out, I resigned, believing ministry was no longer something I wanted to pursue. Those around me could not understand this decision and quickly began to hurl insults and make unfair accusations against me. Even making up lies as to why I left the ministry, which—in my mind—only reinforced my decision to walk away. I quickly took a job in corporate America but soon realized God did not call me into the business world. I was called to help people find Christ and the abundant life he died for them to have. To make a long story short, I quit that job and a few months later, launched Real Life Church. As a result, God not only saved me from myself, he also allowed me the opportunity to continue to partner with him in the saving of others. Only, this time, in a venue better suiting my personality and ministry style.

But that's not the end of my story. In 2018, I was offered the opportunity to merge Real Life Church with Family Church, becoming the lead pastor of both churches. Family Church has a multimillion-dollar facility sitting on twenty acres just outside our city. Each week I speak into the lives of thousands through teaching and writing. I'm proof you can go into the dark and come back out into the light with more than you lost (if you will keep your heart right and your mouth shut)!

PART XII

GOD HAS A PLAN

Jesus replied, "You have said it. And in the future you will see the Son of Man seated in the place of power at God's right hand and coming on the clouds of heaven." (Matthew 26:64 NLT)

"God's plan for your life far exceeds the circumstances of your day." —Louie Giglio

Chaos in Disguise

STARS SHINE BRIGHTEST on moonless nights. You don't need the conditions to be right in order to dump your doubts and have unshakable faith.

Key Verse: "And we know that in all things God works for the good of those who love him, who have been called according to his purpose" (Romans 8:28).

As the darkness closed in, Jesus trusted the plan of God. With only the promise of dawn, the future was his focus. Perhaps he was thinking back to the creation of the earth and how bleak everything appeared before God said, "Let there be light." He knew the cross wasn't a suicide mission; it was a rescue mission. Each passing minute only brought him closer to fulfilling his destiny, but before he could sit down at God's right hand, he would have to lay down his right to a fair trial. You may feel as if life has been terribly unfair to you. Perhaps the blur of what has been has blocked your view of what is to come. As you move through this section, keep in mind stars shine their brightest when night falls. It's the darkness that brings out their beauty, not the light.

Do you ever wonder how Jesus kept it together, as his life fell apart? I do. I've also heard more than my fair share of generic answers. As teachers, we do our best to bring our listeners into

187

the moment. We read the verses and paint a picture as passionately as we can. However, I honestly feel the reality of what Jesus endured somewhat gets lost in translation. I am guilty here. I am not sure it's possible to capture the brutality of the cross from the comfort of the pulpit. Mel Gibson's *Passion of the Christ* is the closest depiction I have seen.

I do know Jesus trusted what God was doing. I think he brought it up at the end, not just to remind his killers of what was to come, but perhaps to remind himself. He needed the reassurance as he confidently stepped off the cliff into the shadows. When life blacks out, your problems get most of the press. What if instead of explaining how crucifixion works, you concentrated more of your time and effort on how God works? Jesus said to the Sanhedrin, "In the future you will see." He wasn't referring to his death. He was proclaiming his return. The cross he faced wasn't his focus. The future he expected garnered his full attention. Like Jesus, you too can prophesy to every harassing thought. You can boldly proclaim to the storm, "In the future you will see."

In the field of physics there is something called chaology. (Basically, it's the study of chaos.) Scientists discovered by studying particles, what looks like chaos on the surface, actually has a pattern with an intended end. They learned how confusion is actually transformational. We don't need a physicist to tell us sometimes the chaos we experience in life really does have a future purpose. What looks like confusion, can actually be the plan of God coming together. There is no better example of this than creation:

> Now the earth was formless and empty, darkness
> was over the surface of the deep, and the Spirit

of God was hovering over the waters. And God
said, "Let there be light," and there was light."
(Genesis 1:2–3)

Not only was the earth dark, it was also empty and formless. To say it was chaotic would be an understatement. Maybe
you can relate to how the earth felt. Hollow and undefined, you
navigate through the chaos of your day without any sense of
direction. If you had a compass to point the way, you would
throw it at your irritators. North, south, east, and west are use-
less coordinates when darkness looms on every side and you're
consumed with restlessness. Blackout can take all meaning out
of life, leaving you to exist in a state of constant confusion.

What if the chaos you're currently experiencing actually
has an intended end? Don't close this book just yet. Hear me
out before you decide I have crossed the line. I understand your
skepticism but maybe there's more going on under the surface
than on the surface. What if, behind the scenes, God intends to
create a beautiful paradise currently unknown to you? What if
your chaos is morphing into a masterpiece? Would that keep
you in the fight?

At creation, a darkness completely devoid of light covered
the earth. Keep in mind: the sun, moon, and stars were not yet
created (Genesis 1:16). The Holy Spirit hovered just above the
inky blackness. The Spirit of God still hovers over the blackness
we experience. Not as a distant deity unplugged from his creation but as a loving father tenderly waiting to announce the
light. There is something about chaos God cannot resist. He is
attracted to it. We tend to avoid those whose lives have fallen
into confusion. After all, we usually have more than our fair
share of problems to keep us occupied. Jesus, however, could not

stay away from those whose lives fell into disarray. Chaos and confusion usually meant an audience with him. It wasn't those who had it all together he sought out. It was those falling apart who brought him running. In a state of utter chaos, the Spirit of God brooded. In this state of turmoil and confusion something wonderful was happening. The earth was transitioning!

Reflection Journal: Today, like Jesus, prophecy to your darkness.

Fear Blocker

"That is why, for Christ's sake, I delight in weakness, in insults, in hardships, in persecution, in difficulties. For when I am weak, then I am strong" (2 Corinthians 12:10).

■ ■ ■

God Works the Nightshift

CREATION WAS PROGRESSIVE. Each day wasn't just a rerun of the day before. It was going somewhere and moving forward. You can move forward as well.

Key Verse: "And God said, 'Let there be light,' and there was light" (Genesis 1:3).

God stood on the balconies of heaven peering down into what most would consider a lost cause. Nothing was alive. Perhaps you have even said that about your situation. The earth was formless, having no definite shape or structure. Does that sound like your life? (It needs to be redefined. A new mold for the future is necessary.) I have tried to imagine this moment in time. I see God, before the earth was created, staring into the empty darkness and thinking to himself, *I smell fresh grass. I taste the saltiness of the ocean on my tongue. I feel the cool wind of winter blowing across my cheeks.* God took what was without shape and formed it into the beautiful earth you and I enjoy today. How? The earth had a "God said" moment.

Genesis chapter one is filled with what God said. God not only said, "Let there be light." He also said, "Let there be man, animals, fish, and plant life." God did not wait for conditions to get better before he spoke the future into existence. While it was still dark, he was imprinting a mold for what was to come. God saw a garden in the gloom. When the stable boundaries of your life give way and a sudden formlessness becomes reality, like the earth, you need a "God said" moment. This is when the Lord stands on the edge of your darkness and calls forth the light.

Unlike so many, God doesn't speak just to hear himself talk. When God says something, it matters, because his words are established in heaven. Everything he spoke in the Genesis account came to pass. The future you seek is only a breath away. However, there are some valuable lessons contained in the creation account that will help you get there. Allow me to explain.

God's days start at night. You probably think about the day starting when you get up in the morning (I know I do), but if you look at the process of how God handled the remaking of the earth, it was just the opposite:

> God called the light "day," and the darkness he called "night." And there was evening and there was morning—the first day. . . . God called the vault "sky." And there was evening, and there was morning—the second day. . . . And there was evening, and there was morning—the third day. (Genesis 1:5, 8, 13)

Each day of creation began with evening (or darkness). It wasn't the sunrise that put God to work; it was the sunset. During the creation of the earth, each new morning revealed what God was working on during the previous night. When you're experiencing the chaos of darkness, God is working! His days start at night. When it's dark we usually go to sleep but not

God. When it's night for you, his day is just beginning. God works the night shift!

King David often spoke about his heart being established in a night season. He understood that at night, people tend to lose their way because this is where confusion exists:

> I will praise the LORD, who counsels me; even at night my heart instructs me. I keep my eyes always on the LORD. With him at my right hand, I will not be shaken." (Psalm 16:7–8)

With each new day, there was always a transition period called night. In order to get to the next new day or the next new thing, you had to keep going once the sun was down. "God said," moments happen in the dark. In regards to creating, God prefers moonlight to sunlight. When you can't see where you're going, don't be alarmed, keep walking. God will build the road as you go.

Reflection Journal: Describe the chaos in your life. Now ask God to turn your misery into a masterpiece.

Fear Blocker

"I sought the LORD, and he answered me; he delivered me from all my fears" (Psalm 34:4).

■ ■ ■

DAY

36

Getting the Conditions Right

THE CREATION OF the earth took six days. When life goes haywire, time becomes a factor. Most can tolerate one or two formless, empty days, filled with crippling anxiety but not six. Stay strong!

Key Verse: "God saw all that he had made, and it was very good. And there was evening and there was morning—the sixth day" (Genesis 1:31).

I have read the creation story hundreds of times. Recently, while teaching on the excellence of God, I discovered something I should have recognized all along. I often invite my audience to participate with me as I teach. One Sunday morning someone asked, "Why did God wait until the sixth day to create man? If man was created to be in charge of the earth shouldn't Adam have been around while God was putting everything together?" Without even thinking about my response, the Holy Spirit prompted me and I said, "God first had to create conditions capable of sustaining life. The atmospheric composition around the earth had to be perfectly in tune with what mankind needed in order to survive. God knew for man to thrive he needed water, food, and sleep cycles. God waited to create man until everything was in place for his success." (Thank you, Holy Spirit, for that smarter-than-me answer!)

God could have created Adam and Eve on the first day, but they wouldn't have lived very long in conditions not yet survivable. Because he loved them and wanted them to have the best shot at life, God waited.

If you feel like your stay in the dark has been overextended, remember God is creating conditions crucial to your success. He is arranging the very things you will need if you're going to thrive and enjoy the future. He isn't being cruel or punishing you. He only wants what's best for you and sometimes what is best is last to arrive. The prophet Isaiah knew a thing or two about the importance of waiting on God. Listen to his advice on how to receive fresh strength:

> Don't you know anything? Haven't you been listening? GOD doesn't come and go. God lasts. He's Creator of all you can see or imagine. He doesn't get tired, doesn't pause to catch his breath. And he knows everything, inside and out. He energizes those who get tired, gives fresh strength to dropouts. For even the young people tire and drop out, young folks in their prime stumble and fall. But those who wait upon GOD get fresh strength. They spread their wings and soar like eagles, they run and don't get tired, they walk and don't lag behind. (Isaiah 40:28–31 MSG)

While God is not the author of confusion (1 Corinthians 14:33), he will use our confusion and turmoil to take us into a brighter tomorrow. Isaiah was right, God doesn't get tired and he doesn't need to catch his breath. You, however, might be winded and weak. Fresh strength isn't for those who work their way through their problems apart from God. That leads to burnout. Fresh strength is for those who fight the good fight of faith even though they feel emotionally drained.

Reflection Journal: Describe the current condition of your life. Can you see God putting the puzzle pieces together? How?

_____

_____

_____

_____

_____

Fear Blocker

"Let us not become weary in doing good, for at the proper time we will reap a harvest if we do not give up" (Galatians 6:9).

■ ■ ■

Part XII

Beacons of Light

- "Through him all things were made; without him nothing was made that has been made. In him was life, and that life was the light of all mankind. The light shines in the darkness, but the darkness has not overcome it" (John 1:3–5).

- "Get out of bed, Jerusalem! Wake up. Put your face in the sunlight. GOD's bright glory has risen for you. The whole earth is wrapped in darkness, all people sunk in deep darkness, but GOD rises on you, his sunrise glory breaks over you" (Isaiah 60:1–2 MSG).

- "He opens up the depths, tells secrets, sees in the dark—light spills out of him!" (Daniel 2:22 MSG).

A Story of Unshakable Faith

After Ashley graduated from high school, she quickly enrolled in Bible college. Young and full of excitement for the future, her dream of full-time ministry was finally in sight. A setback was the last thing on her mind. "I didn't understand why I was getting so sick all the time. After all, I was in the place God had called me and I felt like I was in the middle of his will. The constant stomach and back pain weren't just keeping me from enjoying life, they were draining the life out of me. I was a physical and emotional wreck," she said. By the time the second semester of college rolled around, Ashley's life was in a full downward spiral. In spite of the tremendous pain, doctors were unable to find anything physically wrong with her. At her lowest point, she was convinced the pain in her body was never going to subside.

"I remember sitting in a Wednesday night prayer service at church. The pain was significantly higher. I felt like someone was stabbing me in the stomach repeatedly with a knife. I went home. I will never forget lying on the bathroom floor sobbing, screaming, and crying out to God for help. I was at the end of what I could take," she explained.

She went back to the emergency room, and this time, the doctor ordered a CT scan, revealing a large golf ball sized polyp in her small intestine that was about to burst. She suffered extreme blood loss during surgery and had to have part of her small intestine removed. From a medical standpoint, she should have lost her life that night. The days to follow were dark. With a tube down her throat, they waited to see if her stomach would heal. To everyone's amazement, Ashley made a full recovery. While doctors and modern medicine redefined the condition of her sick body, God was redefining her character and walk with him. Listen as Ashley explains what was happening to her spiritually as she trusted the plan of God.

"I did not know at the time that God would use my illness to transform my life and shape my faith. I learned firsthand what spiritual warfare feels like. All I can say is that in the deepest, darkest, hardest, and most exhausting point in my life, I learned that God is so, so, so good! I can now impact his kingdom in ways that would have been impossible without the struggle. I am thankful for God's plan and for not giving up, when giving up was all I wanted to do. Every breath that we take here on the earth is for a purpose, God's purpose."

God used the chaos in Ashley's life to create the future he had in mind for her all along.

PART XIII
BROKEN TO BE BLESSED

*Near the cross of Jesus stood his mother,
his mother's sister, Mary the wife of Clopas,
and Mary Magdalene. When Jesus saw his
mother there, and the disciple whom he loved
standing nearby, he said to her, "Woman, here
is your son," and to the disciple, "Here is your
mother." From that time on, the disciple took
her into his home. (John 19:25–27)*

*"The world breaks everyone, and afterward,
some are strong at the broken places."*
—Ernest Hemingway

Change of Address

WHEN WHAT MATTERS most is lost, it can become the source of your greatest worry. A broken heart is often the result of absence. Today, refuse to breakdown, by pressing into your breakthrough.

Key Verse: "His kingdom will never end" (Luke 1:33b).

It's hard to imagine what was going through Mary's mind as she witnessed the crucifixion of her son. John describes her as standing near the cross of Jesus but in the original manuscript, it states she was standing by his cross. Mary could not be kept away. I see her, on her knees under the hanging body of her firstborn, hands in the sand wet with his blood. Tears are falling and she has a broken heart full of questions. As a father and grandfather, I cannot fathom the depths of her pain nor the level of her anxiety. I don't have the vocabulary to describe to you the extent of her brokenness. Nobody does.

Perhaps her mind drifted back to the night the angel of the Lord first appeared to her explaining the birth of Jesus. The heavenly messenger boldly proclaimed, "His kingdom will never end" (Luke 1:33). Yet it was ending or at least appeared to be. There was no mention of the cross as they planned for the cradle, no talk of crucifixion, only divine conception (Luke 1:35). Is this your story? Has the source of your happiness become the source of your greatest pain? Are you upset and crashing because something of value was unfairly taken?

For thirty-three years Mary witnessed the miracle-working power of Jesus. She was there as he bent the laws of nature and demonstrated power over death. She, of all people, knew he could climb down off the cross proving once and for all he was God. Knowing this only added weight to the mountain of hurt already crushing her. Why was this happening? It wasn't supposed to turn out like this but somehow it did. While Mary had other children (Matthew 12:47), none were as special as Jesus. He was more than a son. He was the promised Messiah. Nothing she possessed was of more value than he.

When something or someone important to you is suddenly gone or unfairly ripped away, the result is an ever-consuming emptiness. How you choose to fill that void will greatly impact the direction of your life. Like Mary, you too can find the hope and strength needed to move forward. While you can never replace what was taken, your life can be full again. There is hope when your heart is broken. The prophet Hosea wonderfully explains how God can restore our lives no matter the severity of our circumstances:

> "I'll give her bouquets of roses. I'll turn Heartbreak
> Valley into Acres of Hope." (Hosea 2:15a MSG)

Are you living in Heartbreak Valley? If so, you're perfectly positioned for something brand-new to happen. According to the prophet, God can turn a gut-wrenching valley of despair into acres of rejoicing. How did Mary change her spiritual address? How did she go from Heartbreak Valley to Acres of Hope? In my opinion, if you are looking up at a crucifixion, you are in a perfect position to make eye contact with Jesus.

Reflection Journal: God wants to change your spiritual and emotional address. What do you want your new location to look like?

_____

_____

_____

_____

_____

Fear Blocker

"God is our refuge and strength, an ever-present help in trouble. Therefore we will not fear, though the earth give way and the mountains fall into the heart of the sea, though its waters roar and foam and the mountains quake with their surging. There is a river whose stream make glad the city of God, the holy place where the Most High dwells. God is within her, she will not fall. God will help her at break of day" (Psalm 46:1–5).

■ ■ ■

Don't Pull Away

JESUS KNEW A broken heart is pulled back together by family and friends. There are no Lone Rangers in the kingdom of God. You conquer worry by surrounding yourself with the right people.

Key Verse: "Jesus saw his mother and the disciple he loved standing near her. He said to his mother, 'Woman, here is your son.' Then to the disciple, 'Here is your mother.' From that moment the disciple accepted her as his own mother" (John 19:26–27 MSG).

When your heart is broken, it's easy to isolate. You can even pull away from those closest to you. This creates a difficult-to-escape bubble of pain. In therapy, I have listened as those surrounded by family and friends declare their loneliness. They say things like, "I am living in a glass house absent of air. I feel like everyone is standing outside watching me silently suffocate." I tell them, "When you wall yourself in by pushing everyone else out, there is nothing left to do other than marinate in your pain. You're not a victim nor a martyr, and nothing is gained when you decide to go it alone."

This approach may seem harsh and without empathy, but it is better than allowing them to live unquestioned on an island of despair. Jesus was going to make sure this did not happen to his mother. Mary needed the support of others and so do you. While you may feel deserted, rarely are you truly by yourself. If you took an honest look at your life, I bet you'd discover many people standing at the foot of your cross. Isolation is a choice, your choice. Mary did not refuse to be comforted by the company of others. She wasn't going to make a terrible situation worse by alienating herself nor would she withdraw into a cocoon of self-pity and depression.

It is universally accepted by biblical scholars, both ancient and modern, the disciple whom Jesus loved was the apostle John. After the crucifixion, John took Mary into his home and she became a part of his family. Keep in mind, at the cross, Jesus's mother was surrounded by three other women, and while their help during crisis was meaningful, Jesus wanted to ensure future support for her as well. Perhaps he remembered the lonely nights in the garden when he felt alone while the disciples slept. Solomon said, "It is better to have a partner than go it alone" (Ecclesiastes 4:9 MSG), and he was right. God said, "It is not good for the man to be alone" (Genesis 2:18). When you decide to push everyone away, you're playing right into the enemy's hands. The banana leaving the bunch gets peeled!

Consider the people in your life right now God has provided to support you during this difficult period. Has the level of your pain caused you to overlook them? Have you decided that since they have never been through what you're experiencing, they are of no real help? Remember, John was an unlikely candidate to take care of Mary. After all, she had other sons and they would have been responsible for her livelihood. Not to mention the fact John, as far as we know, never lost a child. He could in no way relate to what Mary was feeling, yet he was the one Jesus chose to provide for and look after his mother.

Perhaps you have overlooked John. Who is standing near you? Who has God strategically placed in your life to hold your hand right now? Have you allowed them inside your bubble of pain? Take a moment to consider how you have either pulled them close or pushed them away.

Reflection Journal: Jesus provided John for Mary. Who has Jesus provided for you?

_____

_____

_____

_____

_____

Fear Blocker

"Though an army besiege me, my heart will not fear; though war break out against me, even then I will be confident" (Psalm 27:3).

It's Not the End

MARY DIDN'T PULL the covers over her head and wish away the pain. She took her broken heart with her as she went. Sometimes you have to say to yourself, "Broken heart, pack a suitcase, you're coming with me."

Key Verse: "When the Sabbath was over, Mary Magdalene, Mary the mother of James, and Salome brought spices so that they might go anoint Jesus' body" (Mark 16:1).

The cross wasn't the end of Mary's story, and your problems don't have to be the end of yours. Later, we find her not cowering behind locked doors like the disciples but at the tomb of Jesus. The darkness she endured apparently rattled her faith and drove her back to the graveyard on the third morning. Mary brought more than spices that day, she also brought a wounded heart in need of healing. With all she went through, it is difficult to comprehend what she was hoping to find at the tomb.

Her story teaches us a wonderful lesson. The funeral she thought she was attending exploded into a new beginning simply because she showed up. When life blacks out, you can't stop showing up. The temptation is to push the pause button and checkout. While your heart may be broken, your legs are fine. You must keep going.

I am sure when Jesus was a child, even he scraped a knee from time to time. Mary no doubt bandaged a few bumps and bruises along the way. Now, Jesus would apply bandages to her. Not on the outside but on the inside. You can't see broken hearts. David explains:

> He heals the heartbroken and bandages their wounds. He counts the stars and assigns each a name. Our Lord is great with limitless strength; we'll never comprehend what he knows and does. God puts the fallen on their feet again. (Psalm 147:3–6a MSG)

Wow! You count your problems, while God counts the points of light he will use to guide you out of them. The psalmist was writing about the rebuilding of Israel (Psalm 147:2) but he could have just as easily been writing about Mary—and you. Like Mary, you have to decide to get back on your feet. She wasn't reclining on the couch on the third morning. Her feet took her to the place of resurrection. God will put you back on your feet again once you decide to stop entertaining thoughts of distress. It's time to rise and start moving in the direction of your miracle. You may think you're not ready but remember, God is looking at your heart (1 Samuel 16:7). He alone can see into the intricate layers of who you really are. Better yet, he can see who you have become. This gives him a unique insight and perspective on how to best heal you at the broken places.

God doesn't know you by physical characteristics. A chiseled physique, clear skin, or a beautifully groomed head of hair doesn't interest him. God knows you by what your heart looks like. This approach is very different than the world we live in. All we can see is the outward appearance. We identify those we know and don't know by the features of their face. God isn't like that. Imagine how different life and church would be if we saw each other from God's vantage point! I have a feeling some of the most physically attractive would lose their appeal and Captain Holier-Than-Thou would become Hypocrite-in-Chief.

Even if you don't feel ready to be healed of your brokenness, at least be willing. In all probability, Mary wasn't ready either. Your readiness (or lack of) will only be the deciding factor if you believe the depths or your darkness are greater than the expanse of God's light. God longs to heal you, but you must invite the healing. If you haven't done that yet, why not take a moment and allow him to begin bandaging your wounds.

Reflection Journal: Tell God where it still hurts. Be willing to be healed, even if you're not yet sure how you'll ever get there.

Fear Blocker

"I have told you these things, so that in me you may have peace. In this world you will have trouble. But take heart! I have overcome the world" (John 16:33).

■ ■ ■

A New Identity

HAVE YOU EVER wondered what happened to Mary? Did she spend the rest of her life pining away in a small room in the back of John's house? Did she become the story of tragedy others used as an example of what happens when life is too hurtful? Did she worry herself to death? She could have easily slipped into a state of depression, never to be heard from again. This was not the case. After her heart was broken, Mary decided to live.

Key Verse: "They all joined together constantly in prayer, along with the women and Mary the mother of Jesus, and with his brothers" (Acts 1:14).

After Jesus returned to heaven (Acts 1:9), Mary went to Jerusalem with the disciples to attend a prayer meeting. We find her in the center of what would become one of the church's greatest hours. Mary was in the Upper Room the day the Holy Spirit came! After her heart was broken at the cross, after Jesus left her and went back to heaven, Mary continued to live a full and productive life. Instead of becoming poor old Mary, mother of a crucified son, she became one of the first to have an encounter with the Holy Spirit. She refused to allow what she went through to become her identity. Luke, the writer of Acts, offers this bit advice: "For in him we live and move and exist" (Acts 17:28a NLT).

It's because of him (Jesus) you can live after experiencing the pain of something devastating. He is the reason for your rejoicing. Mary could have missed out on what was no doubt the pinnacle of her spiritual life had she checked out. Now, the same Jesus who once occupied her womb, permeated through every square inch of her body. She was filled with his Spirit. Her decision to identify with Jesus rather than identify with her crisis was the deciding factor. She was full—not with darkness but with Jesus. Mary's journey with Jesus took her from the womb to the tomb to the Upper Room. Had she stopped at the tomb, life for her would not have turned out so wonderful. She had to keep going and so do you.

You too can live, move, and exist in him. Your crisis doesn't have to define the present or become the boundaries of the future. Mary went on to Pentecost. You can go on to whatever lies ahead of you as well. Decide to go on. God has not forgotten you nor will he leave you to figure life out on your own. Your hope cannot be canceled by a broken heart. Your hope lives because Jesus lives.

Reflection Journal: Now that you've finished your 40-day journey, how will you, like Mary, go on to the new things God is doing in your life right now? Be specific.

Fear Blocker

"You will keep in perfect peace him those whose minds are steadfast, because they trust in you" (Isaiah 26:3).

※ ※ ※

Part XIII

Beacons of Light

- "Because of the tender mercy of God, by which the rising sun will come to us from heaven to shine on those living in darkness and in the shadow of death, to guide our feet to the path of peace" (Luke 1:78–79).

- "Commit your way to the LORD; trust in him and he will do this: He will make your righteousness shine like the dawn and the justice of your cause like the noonday sun" (Psalm 37:5–6).

- "For the commandment is a lamp and the teaching a light" (Proverbs 6:23a ESV).

Conclusion

NOW THAT YOU can see the sunrise and have prepared yourself for a life no longer dominated by worry, anxiety, and emotional despair, remember—God had a purpose all along. Together, we have learned what you thought was going to destroy you can actually be used by God for a greater good. While God does not invite dark circumstances, he can use them to move his children forward into a brighter future. Tragedy, heartache, and disappointment happen to everyone, but not many learn to benefit from them. Few become stronger at the broken places. That, in part, is why I wrote this book. God wastes nothing, not even your tears. Congratulations, you made it! You don't have to be completely over it to be through with it.

King David had a unique perspective when it came to the gloomy moments of life. Instead of skipping over the hard stuff, he put his hope in God and pushed through. As you read his writings (Psalms) it quickly becomes apparent David believed that no matter where he was or what he was experiencing God was right beside him. He saw the darkness not as something to destroy him but as God's shadow cast over him:

> Have mercy on me, my God, have mercy on me,
> for in you I take refuge. I will take refuge in the
> shadow of your wings until the disaster has passed.

> I cry out to God Most High, to God, who vindi-
> cates me. (Psalm 57:1–2)

David knew if God could turn night into day, he could also turn his burden into a blessing. For example, the shadow of Goliath would have been a calamity for most of us. David, however, saw it as more of an opportunity. His greatest victory happened in the shadow of a monster (blackout). David lived his entire life in the shadows. Believing the darkness cast in his direction was really more of exit into the light. He took refuge in God until the disaster passed. What if, in the future, you took this same approach and instead of saying, "I am stuck in the dark," you began saying, "I am taking refuge in God's shadow?" Proper perspective changes everything. Hope is working overtime on your behalf.

Once biblical hope is deeply rooted in your life, you will not be so easily moved. The writer of Hebrews describes hope as an anchor (Hebrews 6:19). We tend to drift when the storms of life are pushing against us. Hope keeps us stable in turbulent seas. You can be chained to your pain or you can be anchored in God's promises. There is no middle ground. The prophet Jeremiah offers this insight:

> "But blessed are those who trust in the LORD and have made the LORD their hope and confidence. They are like trees planted along the riverbank, with roots that reach deep into the water. Such trees are not bothered by heat or worried by long months of drought. Their leaves stay green, and they never stop producing fruit." (Jeremiah 17:7–8 NLT)

You can trust the Lord with your future. Plant yourself in hope and know he is with you.

CONNECT WITH LARRY DUGGER

 Facebook.com/LarryDugger

 familychurch.tv

TO CONTACT LARRY OR TO BOOK A SERVICE, CONFERENCE, OR SPECIAL EVENT:

 dugg@fidnet.com

 (417) 650-8841